instant
KEYBOARD

instant KEYBOARD

BY GARY MEISNER

QUICK & EASY INSTRUCTION FOR THE IMPATIENT STUDENT

Copyright © 1987 by Hal Leonard Books.
Printed and bound in the United States of America.
All rights reserved.
No part of this book may be reproduced in any form or by
any electronic or mechanical means including information
storage and retrieval systems without permission in
writing from the publisher, except by a reviewer,
who may quote brief passages in a review.
Published by Hal Leonard Books, P.O. Box 13819,
Milwaukee, WI 53213 U.S.A.   First edition.

Library of Congress Cataloging-in Publication Data

Meisner, Gary.
  Instant Keyboard.

  Includes index.
  1. Electronic keyboard (Synthesizer)—Methods—Self-instruction. I. Title.
MT192.8.M   786   87-3512
ISBN 0-88188-624-6

First printing August, 1987

Introduction

Hi and welcome to INSTANT KEYBOARD. Recent advances in the development of electronic keyboards have resulted in features that are easy to use, sophisticated-sounding, and at the same time musically challenging. Best of all, the possibility of making music quickly and enjoyably regardless of your previous musical training can be, without question, a reality.

With the aid of this book you are going to learn about some music basics, have an opportunity to play terrific tunes like "Memory," "Edelweiss," "Endless Love" and "Spanish Eyes," and above all, find out how to have fun with your keyboard.

This book is divided into four main parts. **Part One** takes you on a step-by-step tour of beginning music elements. These music elements are reinforced by being used in interesting tunes, so you'll always have the opportunity for "hands on" experience as you learn. **Part Two** focuses on Automatic Rhythm. The tunes were selected so specific automatic rhythms could be highlighted and expanded upon. **Part Three** provides some musical tools to "dress up" your playing. You'll learn about grace notes, playing an octave higher, and how to make registration changes to name just a few of the playing techniques explained. **Part Four** contains a comprehensive chord chart, which is a handy reference if you choose to play fingered chords.

As you begin your musical journey, keep in mind that there is a tremendous amount of versatility built into most keyboards. As a result, there's probably a good chance that your keyboard has features that will enable you to play music that is pleasing to you.

Turn the page, and let's get started!

Note: *INSTANT KEYBOARD may be used with any make or model of electronic keyboard. Since every model is different, the keyboard features that are the basis of this book are those most commonly found on electronic keyboards. Also, terminology may vary from manufacturer to manufacturer.*

CONTENTS

PART ONE

THE KEYBOARD

Look at the control panel of your keyboard. You'll most likely see a variety of buttons, switches, sliders, and dials . . . a few here, a few there.

DON'T BE OVERWHELMED!

Remember that electronic keyboards vary in the number of available features, so don't be alarmed if your keyboard does not correspond *exactly* to the diagram shown on the next page.

Whether you have a relatively small keyboard with only 32 keys and a few controls, or a rather large keyboard with as many as 61 keys and a great many controls, most keyboards have some basic features in common.

Getting Acquainted

Spend a few moments and locate these features:

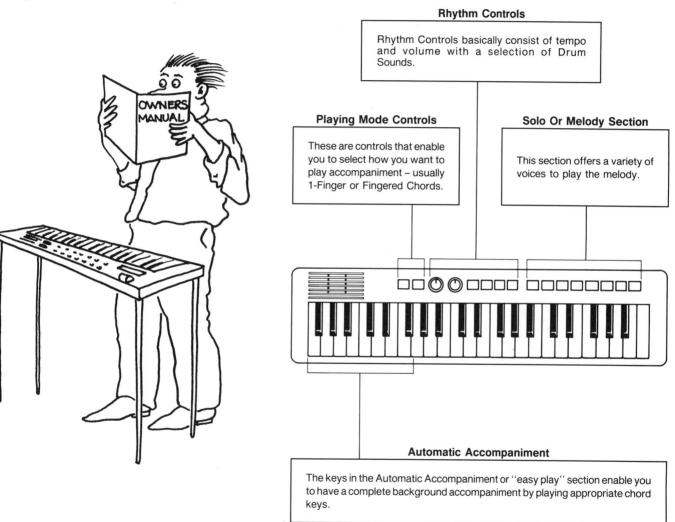

Rhythm Controls

Rhythm Controls basically consist of tempo and volume with a selection of Drum Sounds.

Playing Mode Controls

These are controls that enable you to select how you want to play accompaniment – usually 1-Finger or Fingered Chords.

Solo Or Melody Section

This section offers a variety of voices to play the melody.

Automatic Accompaniment

The keys in the Automatic Accompaniment or "easy play" section enable you to have a complete background accompaniment by playing appropriate chord keys.

TYPICAL CONTROLS

Specific voices and controls from the basic sections of an electronic keyboard are listed in the following . . . you may have more or perhaps less. Whatever the case, survey your voices and controls to determine which of these are available to you and how they are named on your keyboard.

Solo or Melody Section

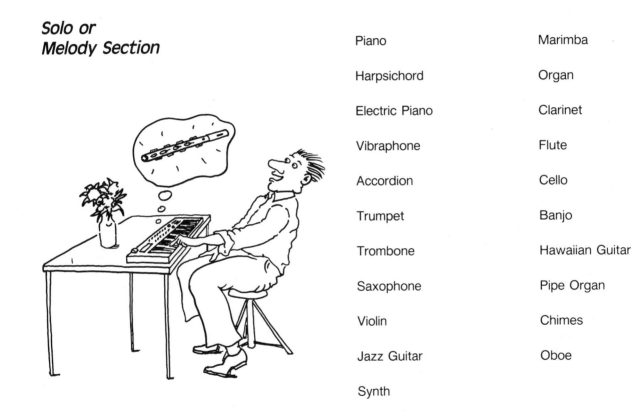

Piano	Marimba
Harpsichord	Organ
Electric Piano	Clarinet
Vibraphone	Flute
Accordion	Cello
Trumpet	Banjo
Trombone	Hawaiian Guitar
Saxophone	Pipe Organ
Violin	Chimes
Jazz Guitar	Oboe
Synth	

Companion Controls: Sustain, Vibrato, Portamento, Pitch Bend, Stereo or Chorus.

Drum Sounds

8 Beat	Disco	Country
Bossa Nova	16 Beat	Tango
Waltz	Slow Rock	Pops
Swing	Samba	Rock

Companion Controls: Tempo, Volume, Start/Stop, Variation, Arpeggio, Fill In and Intro/Ending.

Playing Mode Controls

| 1-Finger Chords | Manual Bass |
| Fingered Chords | Auto Bass Chord |

Companion Controls: Synchro Start/Touch Start/Key Start and Memory.

Balance Controls

Balance or Volume controls enable you to adjust the loudness or softness of individual sections to obtain the best effect. These are your "mixing" controls. The master volume, of course, adjusts the volume of the entire keyboard.

Let's Experiment!

- Select a drum sound, like Swing.

- Press the Start function and listen to the rhythm.

- Listen carefully to all the available rhythms on your keyboard, and adjust the Tempo control to various settings.

- Think of an appropriate tune for as many rhythms as you can, and hum along as the rhythm is playing. It's interesting to note that an appropriate rhythm for a particular tune becomes inappropriate when the tempo is too fast or too slow. Can you imagine what "Love Me Tender" would sound like if you played it at the tempo normally associated with "When The Saints Go Marching In." This indicates a need to adjust the Tempo control carefully for each tune you play.

- Notice the downbeat light, which is also known as a tempo or beat light. This visual metronome typically flashes on the first beat of every measure.

- Now let's complete the automatic accompaniment by activating 1-Finger Chords and Memory (if you have it).

- Press a chord key in the automatic accompaniment section, which is on the left end of the keyboard, and you'll hear a complete professional background that includes bass, accompaniment chords and drums, all synchronized by the drum sound you've chosen. Push a button here, adjust a control there, and you've got a complete accompaniment at your fingertips!

Sequencers

A Special Note About Sequencers:

If your keyboard has a built-in sequencer, it could serve as a useful learning tool in playing any of the songs in this book. Consult your owner's guide for specific information about its operation.

Briefly, a sequencer permits you to record parts of a song separately and then play another part "live" during the playback. For example, you could record the accompaniment chords and then play the melody while the chords are being played back. Or, you could record the melody and then play the chords on playback. The possibilities depend on the number of tracks available on your sequencer. Most importantly, the sequencer can be a useful learning tool in all the music you'll play.

An arrangement of "America" that includes a harmony part is found on pages 84-85.

A FEW MUSIC BASICS

Staff

All of the music in this book is written with easy-to-read notes that name themselves. These notes are placed on a **staff.** The staff consists of five horizontal lines and the four spaces between them. Each line or space represents a lettered note.

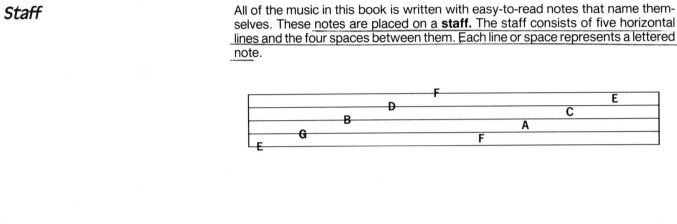

Ledger Lines

Sometimes **ledger lines** are added above or below the staff to accommodate additional notes.

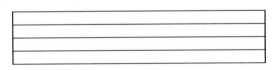

Treble Clef

The squiggly looking sign at the beginning of each staff is called a **treble clef**.

Note Names

Notice that there are only seven note names and that they simply repeat throughout the keyboard. The groups of two and three black keys can be used as guideposts. For example, C is always the first key to the left of the two black keys; F is always the first key to the left of the three black keys.

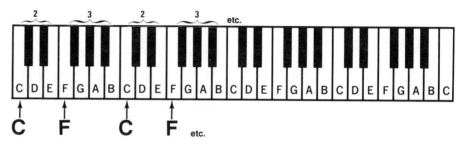

Time Values

Each note not only tells you what key to play but also how long the key has to be held down. This is called the **time value** of the note. Divisions of time in music are called **beats**. Here are four common types of notes and their time values:

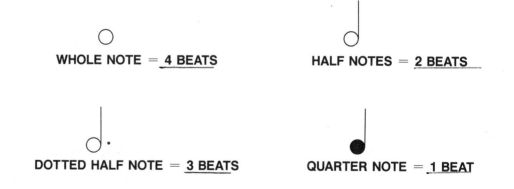

WHOLE NOTE = 4 BEATS   HALF NOTES = 2 BEATS

DOTTED HALF NOTE = 3 BEATS   QUARTER NOTE = 1 BEAT

Keys on the keyboard correspond to notes on the staff. As notes move down the staff, the corresponding keys move down (to the left) on the keyboard. As notes move up the staff, they move up (to the right) on the keyboard.

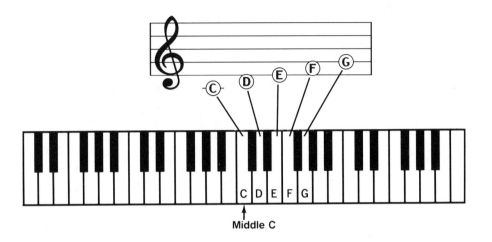

Keyboard Guide Stickers

Place the **Keyboard Guide Stickers,** which are included on the inside front cover of this book, on your keyboard as illustrated. Once you've got the stickers in place, on the sticker itself, draw a circle around the C of Middle C.

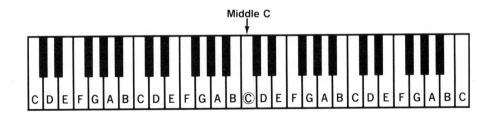

Measures & Bar Lines

Time values in music are grouped into **measures**. Each measure contains a certain number of beats. In written music, measures are separated by **bar lines**.

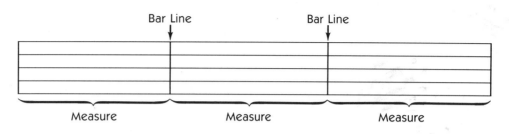

Time Signatures

The constant number of beats between two bar lines is written at the beginning of each tune and is called a **time signature**.

4 beats in each measure

A quarter note gets one beat

The **top number** indicates the number of rhythmic beats in each measure.

The **bottom** number indicates the type of note that receives one beat. 4 indicates a quarter note.

3 Beats in each measure

A quarter note gets one beat

Fingering

The fingers on each hand are numbered. The small numbers that appear above the notes correspond to the finger numbers and suggest which finger to use on each key. To help you get started, finger numbers will be included for most notes.

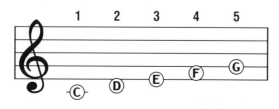

LET'S PLAY A SONG

"Love Me Tender"

Here's your first melody. Before playing:

- Locate these five notes on your keyboard. These are the melody notes for "Love Me Tender," which you play with your right hand.

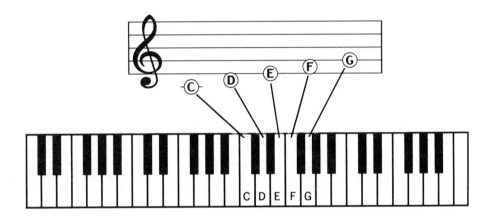

- Select a voice for the melody. Piano is a good choice, if you have it.

- Keep the fingers of your right hand curved, and be sure your thumb is on middle C, with your second finger on D, third finger on E, fourth finger on F, and fifth finger on G. As a matter of fact, spend a few moments and play these notes in random order to get the "feel" of the keyboard.

- Now carefully read the notes and play the corresponding keys with your right hand. If you are familiar with the tune — and you probably are — sing or hum along as you play.

Love Me Tender

Words and Music by
Elvis Presley and Vera Matson

Choosing An Appropriate Voice

Play "Love Me Tender" again. This time, experiment with all of the available voices on your keyboard. You'll find that these voices can be divided into two general groups — tones that sound as long as a key is held down, and tones that fade away. The flute, saxophone, clarinet and trumpet are examples of sounds that are continuous, while the piano, harpsichord and banjo are examples of sounds that fade (decay). Whether a tone is continuous or decays is one important factor in choosing an appropriate melody voice. For example, if a melody has quite a few whole notes (four counts), a banjo voice might not be suitable because the sound would die away before the four counts of a whole note could be completed.

"Regi-Sound Program"

With each song throughout this book, you'll find a heading labeled "Regi-Sound Program." This number corresponds to a number on the Regi-Sound Programs guide at the back of the book. Use these registrations as suggestions only. Never hesitate to experiment on your own.

When The Saints Go Marching In

Regi-Sound Program: 1
Rhythm: Swing

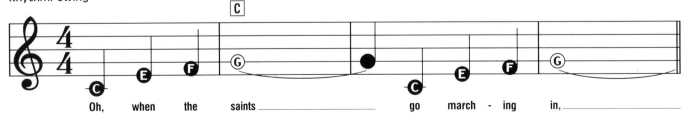

Oh, when the saints   go march - ing in,

Accompaniment

Accompaniment is the chord harmony played by your left hand. In each arrangement, the accompaniment is indicated by boxed chord symbols that appear above the melody. Just match the letter in the box with the chord key in the easy play section of your keyboard. This is 1-Finger Chord Accompaniment.

Another method of playing automatic accompaniment is called Fingered Chords. If you would like to learn this system, turn to page 120.

You'll play three chords in "Love Me Tender" — F, G and C.

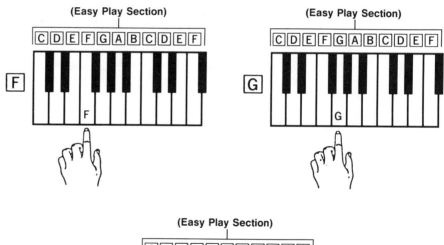

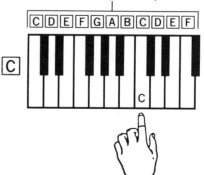

Let's Experiment!

- Set up a Rock or Slow Rock rhythm and start the drums playing.

- Adjust the tempo to a rather slow setting.

- Activate the Memory feature, if you have one. On some keyboards, Memory is automatically programmed. In this mode, you can lift your finger from the chord key and the accompaniment continues.

- Remember, the downbeat light shows you the **first** beat in each measure.

- Look at the music and notice that the flashes of the downbeat light are indicated above each measure.

- If your keyboard has voice tabs for the accompaniment chords and bass, activate at least one voice in each section.

- For now, ignore the melody, and just play the accompaniment chords for "Love Me Tender" as indicated. Count out loud, and let the downbeat flashes guide you.

Love Me Tender

Words and Music by
Elvis Presley and Vera Matson

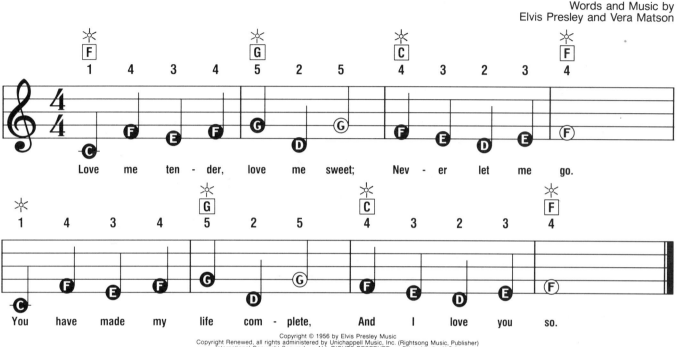

Put It All Together

Play the accompaniment a few more times. Listen carefully to the drums, accompaniment chords and bass. Finally, hum the melody and concentrate on getting the "feel" of the rhythm. The accompaniment is the "glue" that holds the song together.

Most automatic accompaniment units have a control that enables you to place the start of the rhythm "on hold" until you press the first chord key. It is known by various names, like Synchro Start, Key Start, or Touch Start. Before playing the melody and accompaniment together, you may want to play the melody alone a few times. Another optional step is to play the melody with the drum sounds only.

Now play both hands together. Be patient with yourself, and above all, HAVE FUN!

"When The Saints Go Marching In"

Pickup Notes

There are a few new music elements in "Saints." Let's learn about them.

Sometimes the first measure of a song will have an incomplete number of beats. These notes are called **pickup notes**. The last measure provides the missing beats.

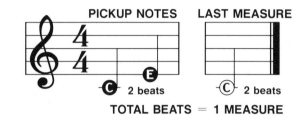

Normally, an accompaniment chord is not indicated until the first complete measure; therefore, the pickup notes are played alone.

Tie

A curved line connecting two notes on the same line or the same space is called a **tie**. A tie indicates that the first note should be played and held for the total time value of both notes.

2 BEATS + 4 BEATS = 6 BEATS   4 BEATS + 4 BEATS = 8 BEATS

When The Saints Go Marching In

Regi-Sound Program: 1
Rhythm: Swing

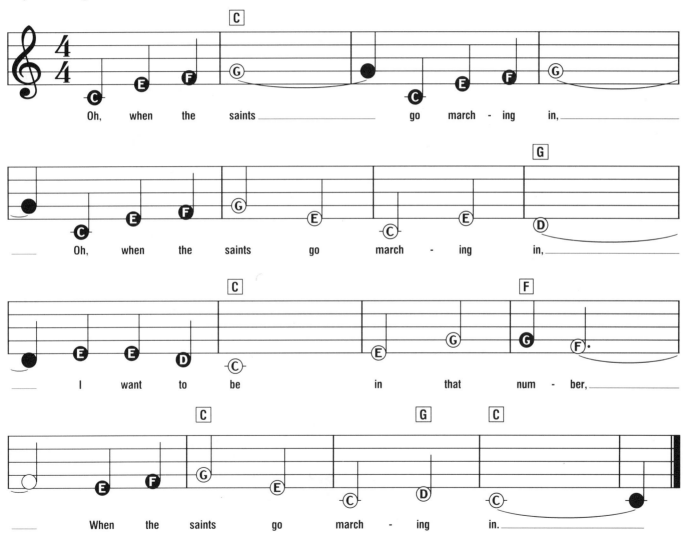

"Supercalifragilisticexpialidocious"

Here's a delightful tune from Walt Disney's MARY POPPINS. Once you feel comfortable playing the melody, don't hesitate to increase the tempo.

New Notes: A,B,C,D

There are some new notes in "Supercalifragilisticexpialidocious."

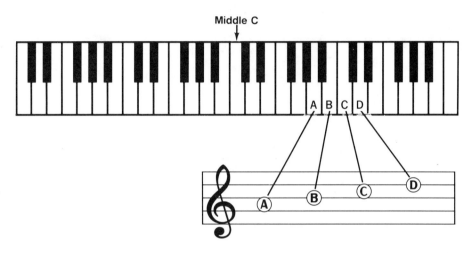

New Fingering Techniques

As the melodies you play increase in the range of notes used, new fingering techniques are helpful in playing smoothly and accurately.

At measure 9, you'll cross your thumb under your second finger.

In measure 12, you'll play A with your second finger and then play the same A in the next measure with your third finger.

Supercalifragilisticexpialidocious

(From Walt Disney's "MARY POPPINS")

Regi-Sound Program: 2
Rhythm: March or Swing

Words and Music by
Richard M. Sherman and Robert B. Sherman

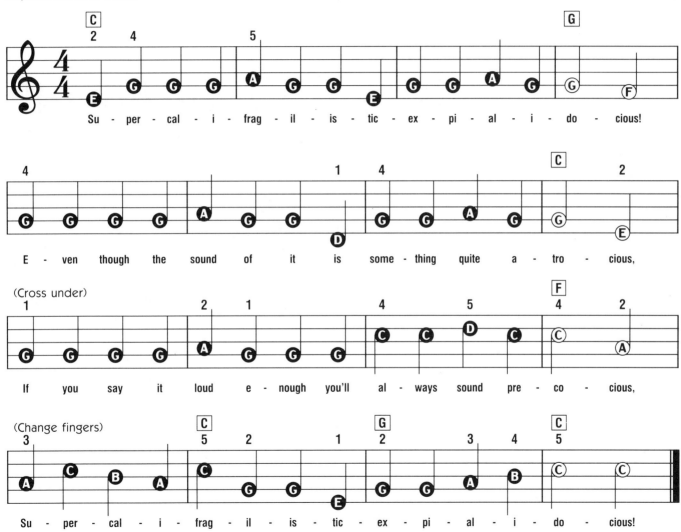

"Chiapanecas"

"Chiapanecas" is the famous hand clapping song often played at sports events. As you play, speed up and slow down to imitate the manner in which this tune is performed when audiences clap their hands.

You'll encounter a few new music elements:

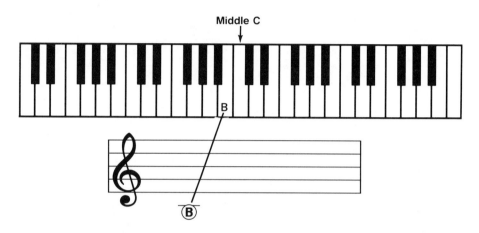

New Note: B

Rests

While notes indicate periods of sound, **rests** indicate periods of silence. When a rest appears, don't play any melody notes.

The quarter rest appears in "Chiapanecas."

Finger Stretch

In the second and tenth measures, you'll have to stretch your fingers a bit to play the notes smoothly. Play these measures a few times without the accompaniment.

Chiapanecas

Regi-Sound Program: 4
Rhythm: Waltz

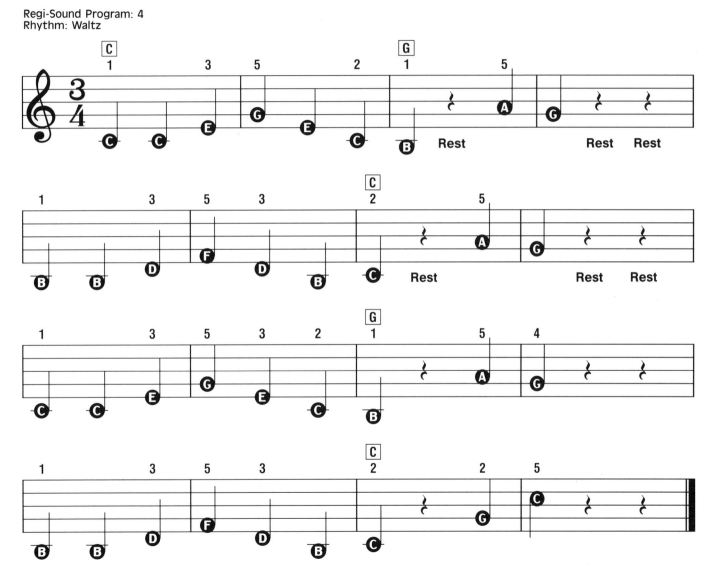

"Memory"

Minor Chords

Up to now you've played just three chords — C, G and F. In "Memory" you'll not only learn some new chords, but chords of a different type. These are **minor** chords, which are indicated with a small "m" to the right of the letter name. For example, the A minor chord symbol looks like this: Am. To play a 1-Finger minor chord, you'll most likely have to press an additional chord key along with the appropriate letter name. Locate and play the new chords Am, Em and Dm. Consult your owner's manual for specific details, if necessary.

If you are playing fingered chords, the chord diagrams for these chords and all others you'll need to play are found in the Chord Chart section, which begins on page 120.

This song is played slowly and has many long notes, so experiment with various voices that don't decay (fade out). Examples of these voices are violin, saxophone, clarinet and oboe.

Memory
(From "Cats")

Regi-Sound Program: 5
Rhythm: Waltz

Text by Trevor Nunn after T.S. Eliot
Music by Andrew Lloyd Webber

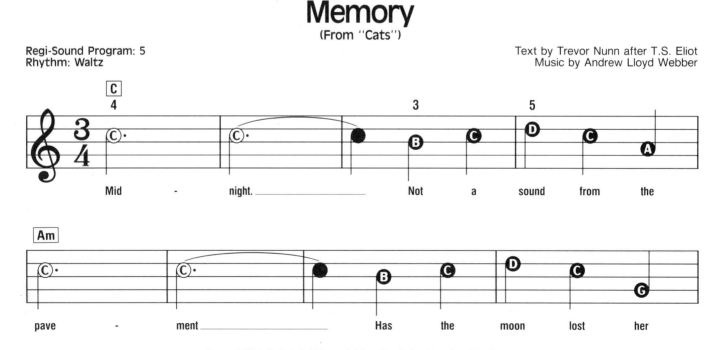

"Edelweiss"

Seventh Chords

There's another new type of chord in "Edelweiss"... it's the **seventh** chord. The seventh chord is indicated with a "7" outside the box, like this: G7. Like minor chords, you'll most likely be required to play an additional chord key along with the appropriate letter name to hear a seventh chord. Locate and play G7 and D7. Keep in mind that seventh chords are always optional, which is the reason that the "7" is placed outside the box. Consult your owner's manual for specific information, if necessary.

Crossing your second finger over your thumb, as indicated in different places throughout the music, will enable you to play the melody smoothly.

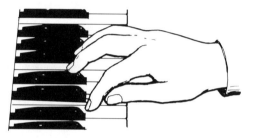

Playing Hints: "Mental Hearing"

We've all experienced a song that is "on our mind" and we can't get rid of it. We find ourselves unconsciously humming it, or whistling it — it drives us crazy! Regardless of how or why it starts, it's a result of mentally hearing a song (in this case, whether we want to or not). It's possible to improve your perception of music and your playing ability, by using **mental hearing** when you practice. It's easy enough to do.

Think about a song you know quite well — for instance, "Edelweiss." You can immediately hear the melody in your mind because it's familiar to you. Your ear anticipates a series of tones in a particular pattern at the mere mention of the title. If you put the music for this song on your keyboard and attempt to play it, you know how the melody should sound; therefore, your familiarity with it enables you to play it as much as your ability to read the music does.

Physically, playing a melody that's set in your mind is much easier than thinking "This is an F, this is a half note," etc. When you can play what you hear in your mind, you'll be playing as a professional does.

What about songs you are not familiar with? Here are some helpful hints:

- **Physically play the music** — first the melody and then the chords (without the automatic rhythm). This involves locating the correct melody and chord keys, trying various fingerings, and incorporating any new musical information.

- **Play the music mentally** — in other words, read it without playing. Try to "hear" the melody in your mind and imagine how each chord sounds as its symbol appears in your music. Humming the melody might be helpful.

- **Set the suggested automatic rhythm and start it playing**. As you listen, watch the music and mentally play the arrangement. As you "hear" the music in your mind, notice how it relates to the drum sounds. In the case of "Edelweiss," you would hear the "boom-chick-chick" of the waltz rhythm.

- **Physically play the melody along with the automatic rhythm;** then do the same with the chord accompaniment part. Finally, put the parts together. When you reach this stage, you are really familiar with the song.

This approach can eliminate quite a few errors you might otherwise make. At the same time, you will make some mistakes—it's part of the learning process. When this happens, don't follow the tendency to stop. Just shake off the error and keep going; this is what the pros do, especially when they are performing with others.

Edelweiss
(From "THE SOUND OF MUSIC")

Regi-Sound Program: 3
Rhythm: Waltz

Words by Oscar Hammerstein II
Music by Richard Rodgers

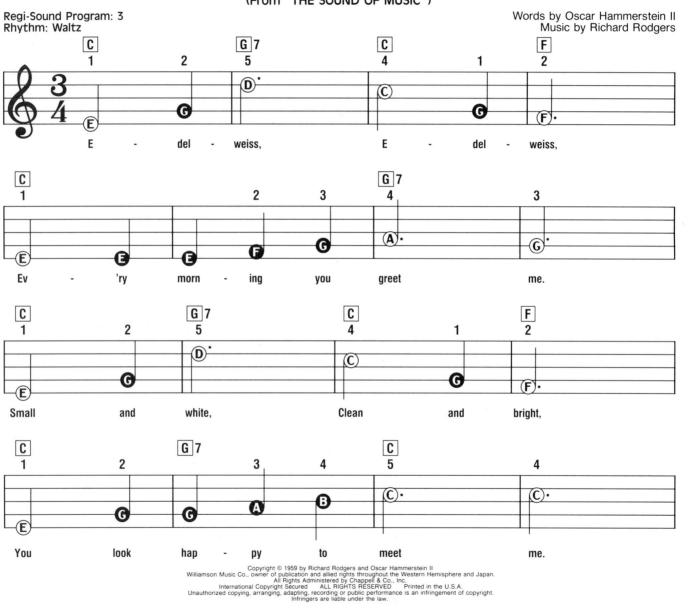

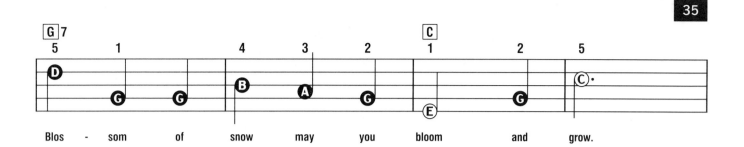

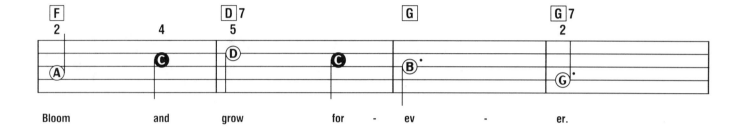

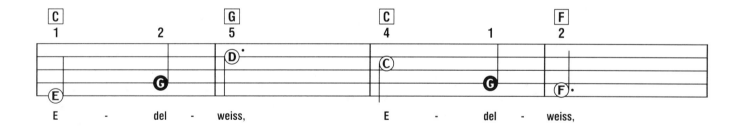

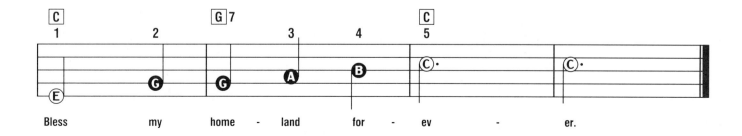

"Village Tavern Polka"

Half Steps

In the "Village Tavern Polka," you'll be playing on a black key for the first time. To understand how black keys are notated on the music, let's learn about **half steps**.

A half step is the distance between any two adjacent keys on the keyboard. Half steps can be formed in three different ways:

Black Key to White Key **White Key to Black Key** **White Key to White Key**

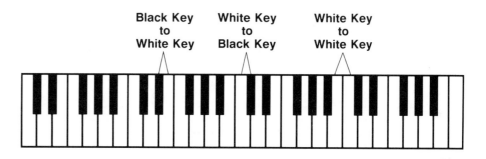

Sharps & Flats

When a **sharp** sign (♯) appears next to any note, raise the note one half step. In other words, play the first adjacent key to the right. When a **flat** sign (♭) appears to the left of any note, lower the note one half step. In other words, play the first adjacent key to the left.

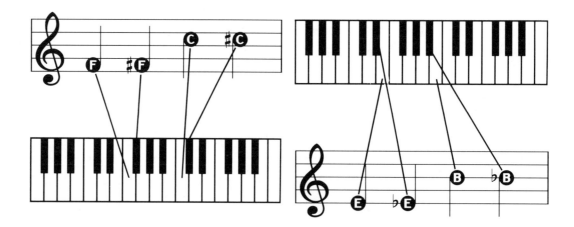

F♯ appears in your new song. Locate and play it.

Village Tavern Polka

Regi-Sound Program: 3
Rhythm: Polka or March

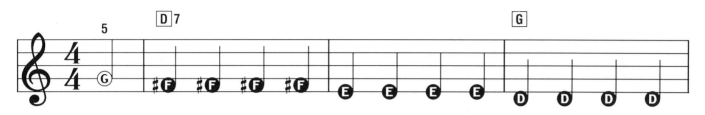

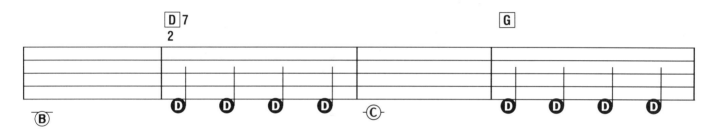

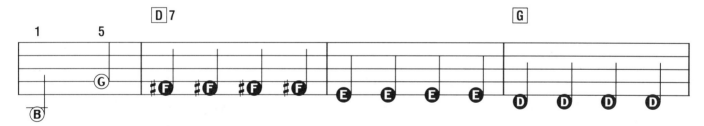

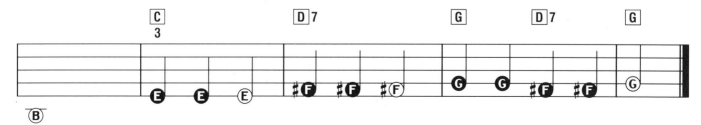

"Alley Cat" & "Wooden Heart"

Repeats

A   B

Repeat signs make it possible for printed music to be shortened without changing the length of the tune.

Generally, repeat signs appear in sets of two.

- There will be one repeat sign (A) at the beginning of the section to be repeated.

- Play up to the repeat sign at the end of this section (B).

- Return to the first repeat sign (A) and play the section again.

- If there is no repeat sign (A), return to the beginning of the song.

When two different endings occur within or at the end of a song, here's what to do:

- Play the song up through the first (1) ending.

- Repeat to the closest repeat sign, or back to the beginning.

- Play that section again, skip the first ending (1), but play the second ending (2).

Alley Cat

Regi-Sound Program: 3
Rhythm: Swing

Music by Frank Bjorn

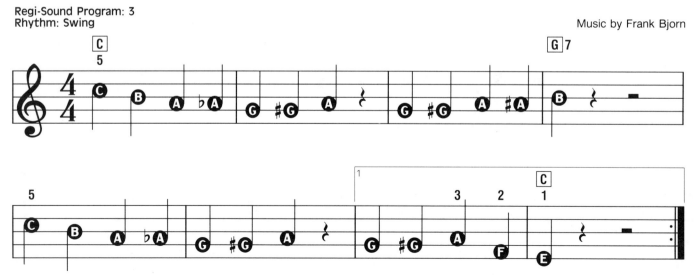

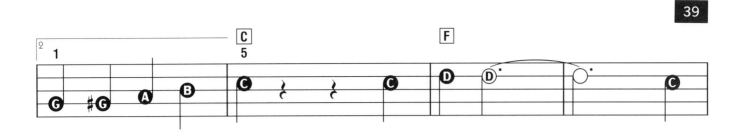
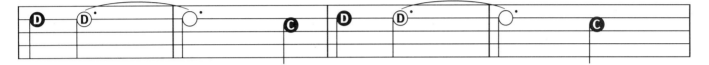
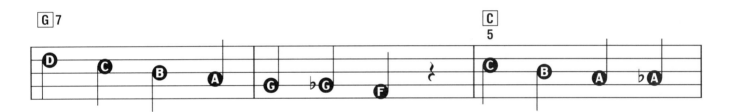
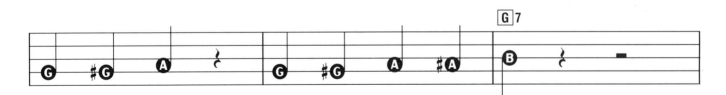

Notice the indication **D.S al Fine** at the end of the song. Just return to the sign (𝄋) and play to fine which means "end."

Wooden Heart

Regi-Sound Program: 2
Rhythm: Ballad or Swing

Words and Music by Fred Wise
Ben Weisman, Kay Twomey
and Berthold Kaempfert

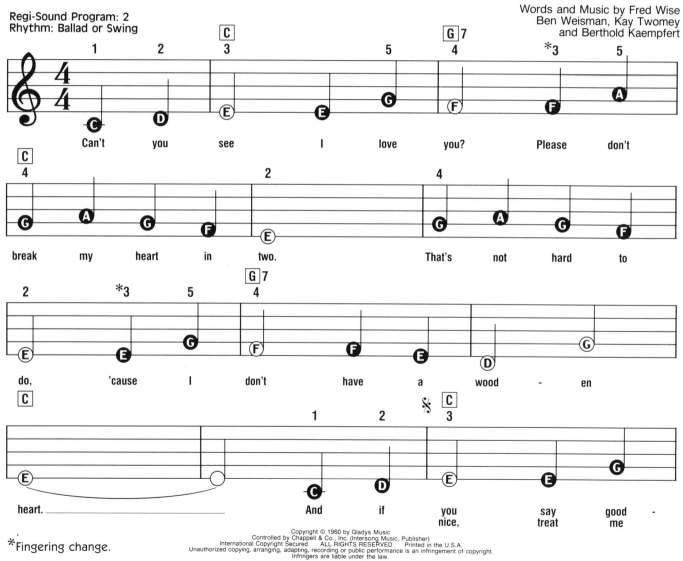

*Fingering change.

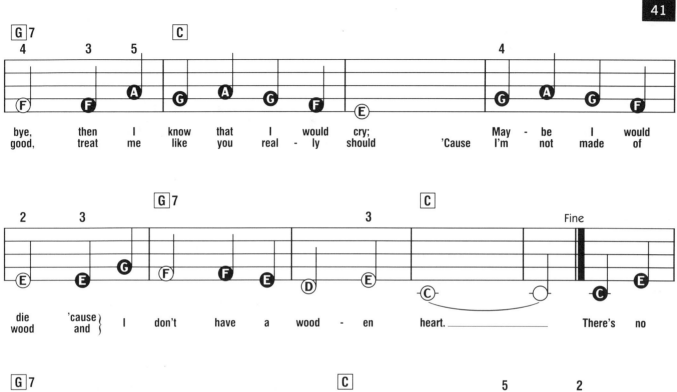

bye, then I know that I would cry;
good, treat me like you real - ly should 'Cause

May - be I would
I'm not made of

die 'cause} I don't have a wood - en heart. _____ There's no
wood and}

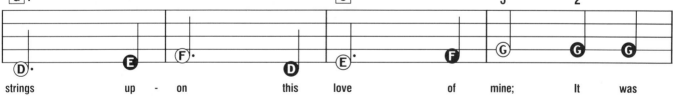

strings up - on this love of mine; It was

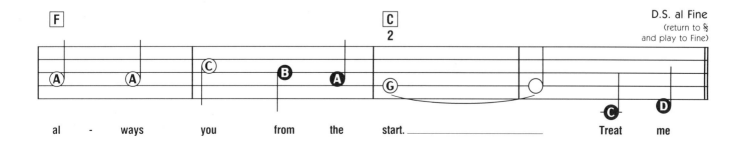

al - ways you from the start. _____

D.S. al Fine
(return to 𝄋
and play to Fine)

Treat me

"Endless Love" & "Every Breath You Take"

New Note: E

There's a new note in "Endless Love."

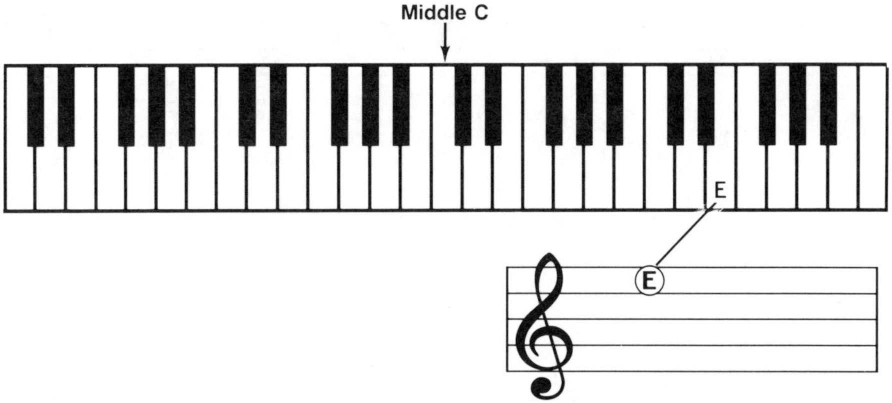

Middle C
E
E

Eighth Notes

Until now, you've played four different types of notes — whole notes, half notes, dotted half notes, and quarter notes. In "Endless Love" and "Every Breath You Take," you'll play **eighth notes**.

When written by itself, an eighth note looks like a quarter note with a flag. Eighth notes written in groups of two or more are connected by a beam.

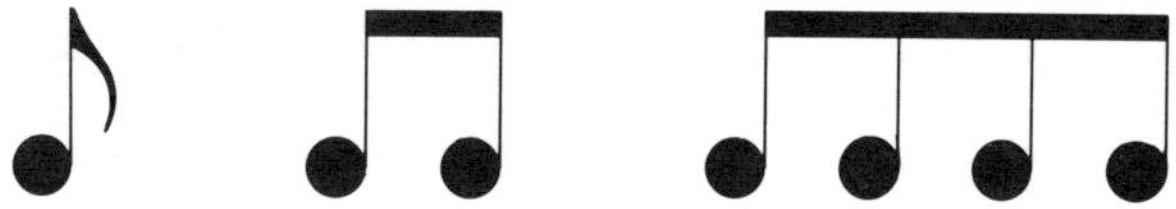

The time value of an eighth note is one-half that of a quarter note. As a result, two eighth notes are equal to one quarter note.

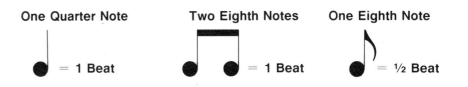

One Quarter Note

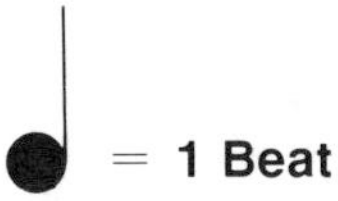

= 1 Beat

Two Eighth Notes

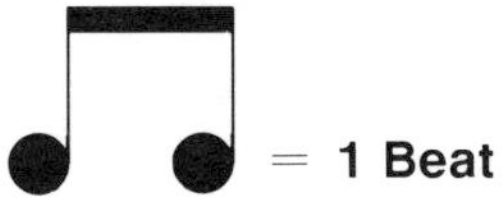

= 1 Beat

One Eighth Note

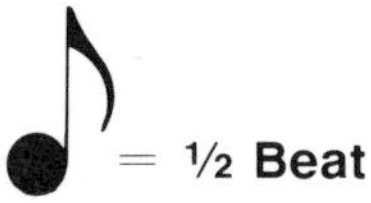

= ½ Beat

The eighth rest also receives one-half count. It looks like this: 𝄾

Because the time value of an eighth note is one half that of a quarter note, each eighth note gets one syllable . . . a number or an "and" (&). Play the following example counting aloud.

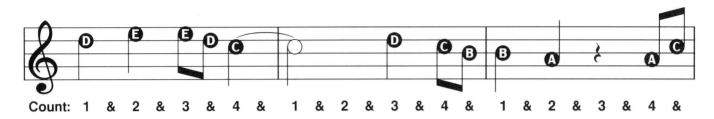

Count: 1 & 2 & 3 & 4 &   1 & 2 & 3 & 4 &   1 & 2 & 3 & 4 &

Dotted Quarter Note

A **dotted quarter** note appears in "Every Breath You Take." To understand the time value of the dotted quarter note, let's return to the dotted half note which you know receives three beats.

A dot placed after **any** note increases the length of that note by one half.

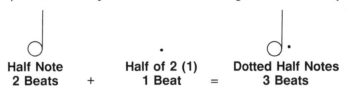

Half Note		Half of 2 (1)		Dotted Half Notes
2 Beats	+	1 Beat	=	3 Beats

The same principle applies to the dotted quarter note.

The dotted quarter note is usually followed by an eighth note.

Quarter Note		Half of 1 (½)		Dotted Quarter Note		
1 Beat	+	½ Beat	=	1½ Beats	1½ Beats	½ Beat

More Finger Substitution

1-3

In "Endless Love" you'll use a finger substitution technique which is made by changing fingers on a key while it is being held down.

Endless Love

Regi-Sound Program: 5
Rhythm: Rock

Words and Music by
Lionel Richie

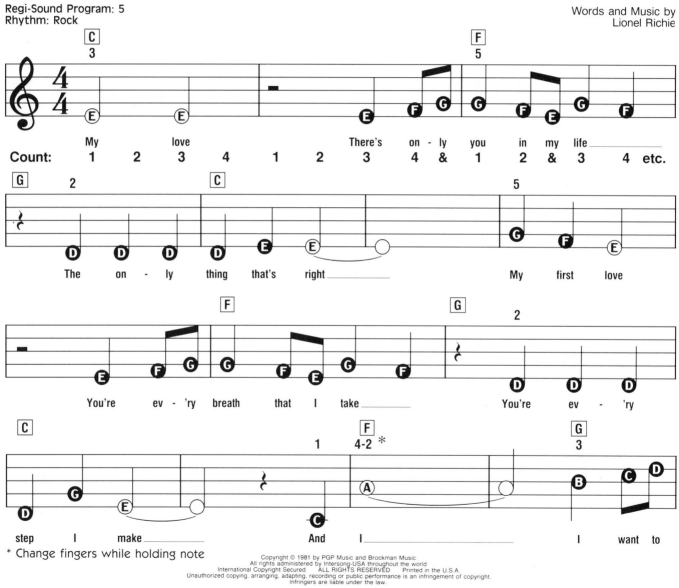

* Change fingers while holding note

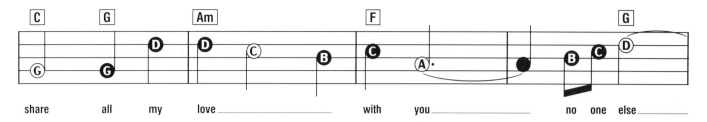

share   all   my   love _____ with   you _____ no   one   else _____

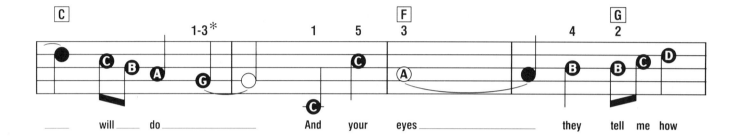

_____ will   do _____ And   your   eyes _____ they   tell   me   how

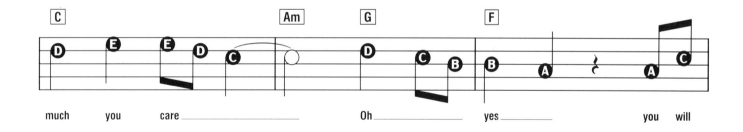

much   you   care _____ Oh _____ yes _____ you   will

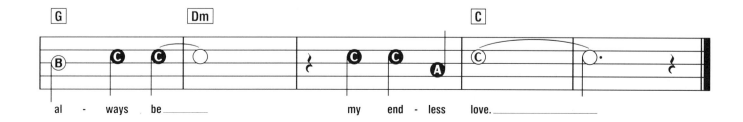

al -   ways   be _____ my   end - less   love. _____

D.S. al Coda is another repeat indication. Return to the (𝄋), which is at the first complete measure of the song; then, skip to the Coda after the first measure of the third line.

Every Breath You Take

Regi-Sound Program: 4
Rhythm: Rock

Words and Music by Sting

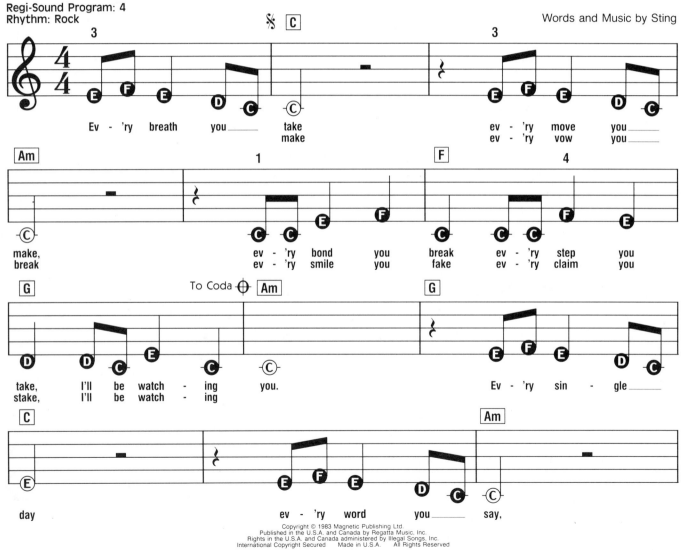

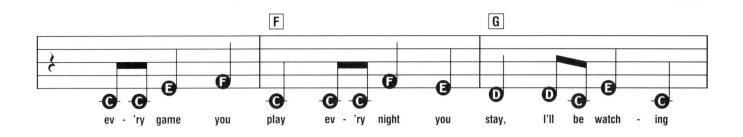

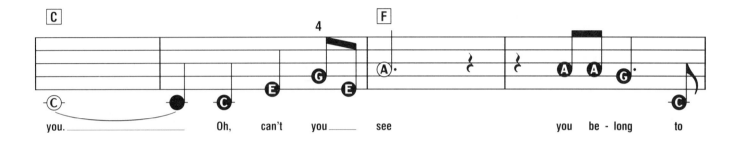

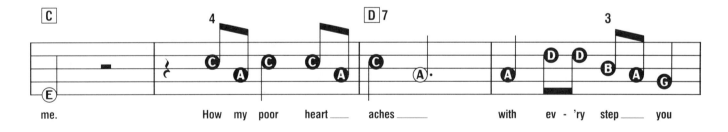

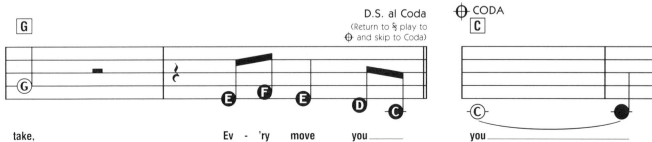

"Spanish Eyes"

New Notes: F, G, A, C

The melody range of "Spanish Eyes" extends beyond that which you've learned in previous songs.

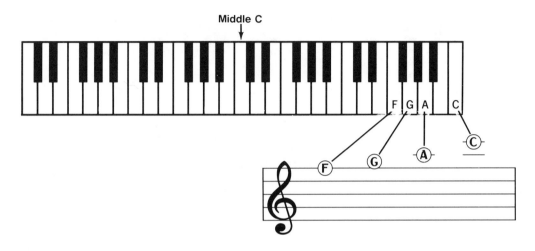

Vibrato

If you have a **vibrato** control, you'll find that it adds a wavering effect to the selected voice creating a warm, lush feeling. Vibrato works well when added to voices like the clarinet, flute, saxophone, violin and oboe. Songs that have some long notes — notes held for four or more counts — lend themselves well to the use of an instrumental solo voice with vibrato. You'll find that the addition of vibrato is perfect for "Spanish Eyes."

Sustain

If **sustain** is available on your keyboard, be sure to try it. Sustain adds a lingering effect to notes after you release them. In this instance play with a short, detached touch.

Gliss

"**Glissando**" is another word in the musical vocabulary; it means "gliding," or "sliding." In everyday use it is often shortened to "gliss."

To play a gliss up the keyboard, turn your hand to the right and use the nail of your index or middle finger to slide across the white keys. Press hard enough to play each note in turn, but slide quickly enough so that the notes blend into a single "whoosh."

Play a gliss down the keyboard by bending your thumb under the palm of your hand and using the thumbnail to play the keys.

A gliss is notated by a wavy line between two notes.

You'll find a gliss indicated in the last two measures of "Spanish Eyes." In the event you don't have the high C note on your keyboard, simply gliss down to Middle C.

Spanish Eyes

Regi-Sound Program: 5
Rhythm: Latin or Rhumba

Words by Charles Singleton and Eddie Snyder
Music by Bert Kaempfert

Blue _____ Span - ish eyes, _____

Tear - drops are fall - ing from your Span - ish eyes, _____

Please, _____ please don't cry, _____

This is just "a - dios" and not good - bye. _____

"He's Got The Whole World In His Hands"

Syncopation

Syncopation is the musical technique of playing certain melody notes on the "weak" beats of the measure. The "strong" beats of a measure are the numbered beats. The "weak" beats are the "and" beats.

Play and count the following examples to hear how the same melody sounds when it's non-syncopated and then syncopated.

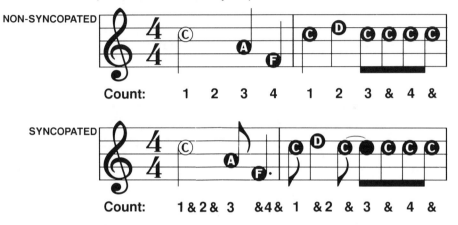

Repeat & Fade

Repeat and fade is a popular recording technique. To create this effect on your keyboard, return to the repeat sign, and play this section again. As you play, use your left hand to gradually reduce the volume in between playing the chords.

He's Got The Whole World In His Hands

Regi-Sound Program: 6
Rhythm: Rock

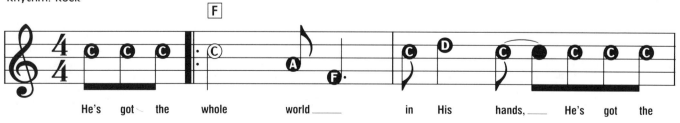

"Yesterday"

New Note: Low A

This all-time hit tune by John Lennon and Paul McCartney introduces a new note, low A, and the minor seventh chord.

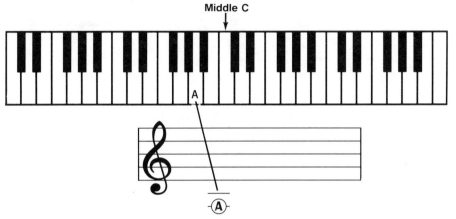

Minor Seventh Chords

The **minor seventh** chord is indicated with an "m" and a "7". To play a 1-Finger minor seventh chord, you'll most likely have to press two additional chord keys along with the appropriate letter name. Locate and play the Bm 7 chord. Consult your owner's manual, if necessary. As with seventh chords, the seventh portion of the minor seventh chord is optional.

Yesterday

Regi-Sound Program: 1
Rhythm: Rock or 8 Beat

Words and Music by
John Lennon and Paul McCartney

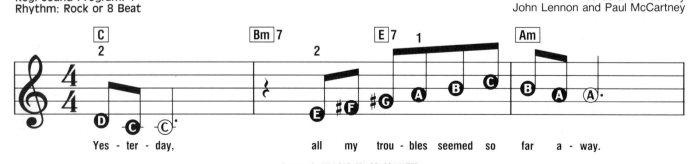

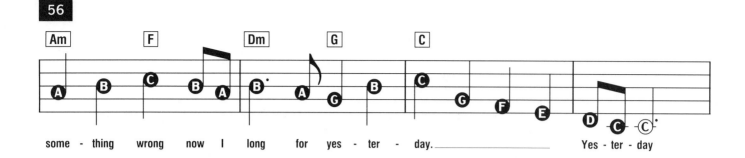

some - thing wrong now I long for yes - ter - day._____ Yes - ter - day

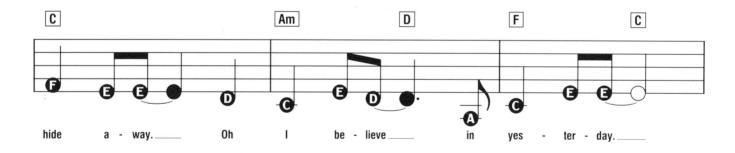

love was such an eas - y game to play. Now I need a place to

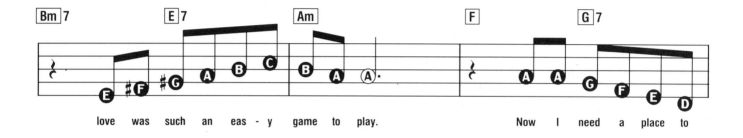

hide a - way.____ Oh I be - lieve____ in yes - ter - day.____

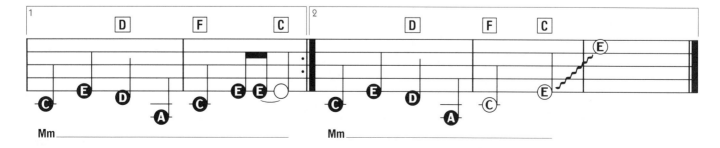

Mm_____ Mm

PART TWO

The "heart" of an electronic keyboard is the **automatic rhythm**. At the touch of a few controls, it's not unusual to hear rhythms that include beautiful, arpeggiated ballads, lively toe-tapping Dixie, electrifying rock, foot stompin' country, and walking bass swing.

Part Two of this book explains the special features of automatic rhythm units and how they can be used in the music you play. In addition, you'll gain "hands on" experience by playing a variety of carefully chosen tunes that focus on specific rhythms such as Bossa Nova, Slow Rock, Swing, and Waltz.

First of all, let's answer the question, "What is **accompaniment**?" Accompaniment, as the word suggests, provides support for the melody. Some instruments — the piano, for example — are capable of producing melody and accompaniment. Think of a pianist playing a ragtime tune like "The Entertainer." Can you picture the left hand of the player moving back and forth between the bass notes and the chords? This is the accompaniment. The melody is played with the right hand. An electric bass, on the other hand, is almost always used to provide a musical foundation — the bass part — for those instruments that play the melody. Specifically, a full accompaniment usually consists of:

- Drums Sounds

- Accompaniment Chords

- Bass

Drum Sounds

The drum sounds consist of snare and bass drums, tom-toms, hi-hat, cymbals, cowbell, maracas, etc. The manner in which those percussion instruments are rhythmically combined and the tempo at which they are played help create the difference between a slow dreamy waltz and a frantic rock rhythm.

A few examples of instruments that play accompaniment chords are the guitar and piano. A guitarist who plays and sings is providing accompaniment chords on the guitar. The acoustic and electric bass, along with the tubas in the marching band, provide most of the bass sounds.

Accompaniment Chords & Bass

When choosing a rhythm for a song, keep in mind that usually there isn't just one that's correct. For example, "Baby Face" was originally introduced as a Fox Trot, and then many years later became equally popular when recorded with a Disco rhythm. "Tea For Two" is another example of a Fox Trot that became a successful Cha-Cha.

Play "Marianne" on the next page using any of the Latin rhythms such as Bossa Nova, Samba, Rhumba, etc., or any of the rock rhythms such as Slow Rock, Jazz Rock, 8 Beat, 16 Beat, etc. Don't forget Swing or Fox Trot.

The point to be made is that **more than one rhythm can be appropriate for a song.**

Marianne

Regi-Sound Program: 2
Rhythm: Experiment!

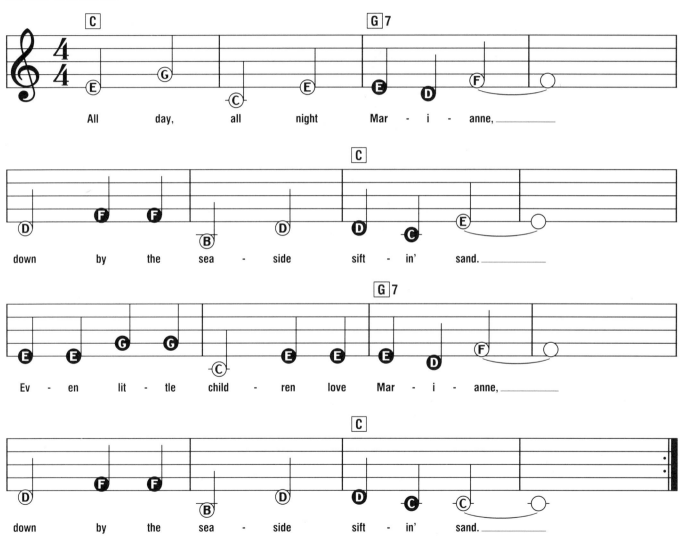

Variation

If you have a **variation** feature, also known as Vary or A/B Vary, you'll find that it usually makes the selected automatic accompaniment more complex. This added rhythmic interest is normally found in the bass and accompaniment chords, while the drum sounds may remain the same. For example, a simple two-beat swing rhythm with the addition of variation may now have a "walking bass" pattern with accompaniment chords on every beat.

Arpeggio

An **arpeggio** can be defined as notes of a chord played one at a time instead of simultaneously. Some instruments on which arpeggios are effectively played are the piano and the harp. If you have this feature, you'll find that it normally works in conjunction with the automatic rhythm. Appropriate background patterns are created for each rhythm. On some keyboards the arpeggio feature is built into certain rhythms and simply comes on automatically.

A few measures of a typical arpeggio pattern are shown in the following music example to give you a visual impression of the arpeggio.

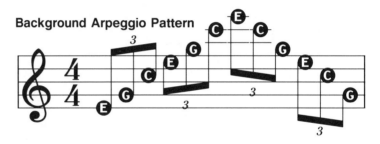

The arpeggio is most effective on songs that have primarily long notes — slow waltzes like "Edelweiss," for example.

Fill

A **"fill,"** as its name implies, usually fills up places in a song where there are rests or where there are long notes. These musical fills can occur in at least two ways:

- The drum solo or break that involves percussion sounds only. (The "break" may also serve to shut off automatic accompaniment.)

- The melodic fill often heard from someone playing a piano or violin in a country/western band.

In some instances, the fill feature may be a combination of the above. A button, tab, or touch-sensitive strip is the usual activating control.

A control marked **Intro/Ending** functions like the fill in that it also provides rhythmic variation. Consult your owner's manual for details about these features.

BOSSA NOVA

Other appropriate rhythms are Latin, Rhumba and Beguine.

Letting the automatic accompaniment run before starting a song in the Latin American vein makes an ideal introduction. Begin with the drum sounds alone for four or eight measures; then, add the chords and bass. Watch the downbeat light, and begin when you're ready.

A Day In The Life Of A Fool
(Manha De Carnaval)

Regi-Sound Program: 1
Rhythm: Bossa Nova

Words by Carl Sigman
Music by Luiz Bonfa

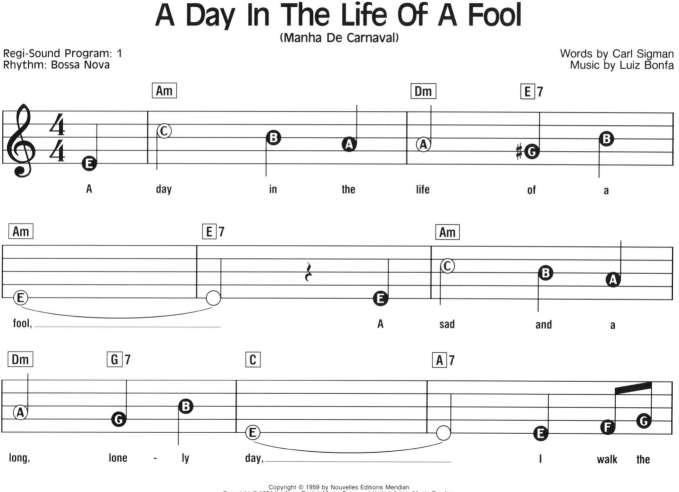

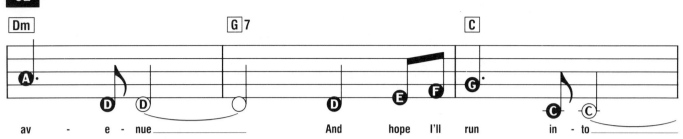

av - e - nue _____ And hope I'll run in - to _____

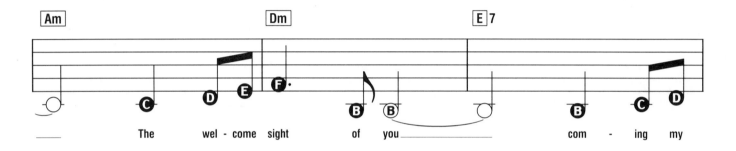

_____ The wel - come sight of you _____ com - ing my

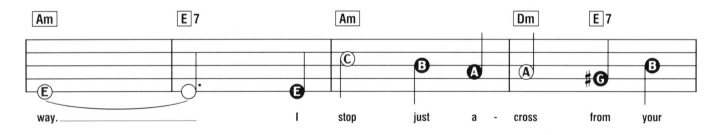

way. _____ I stop just a - cross from your

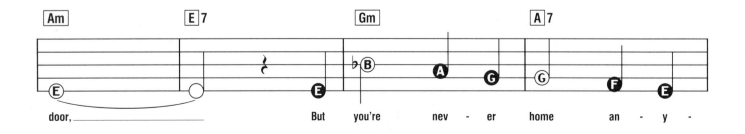

door, _____ But you're nev - er home an - y -

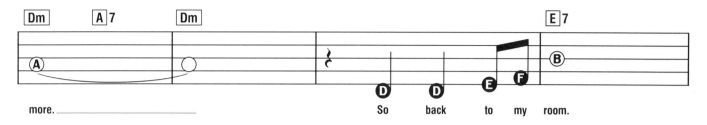

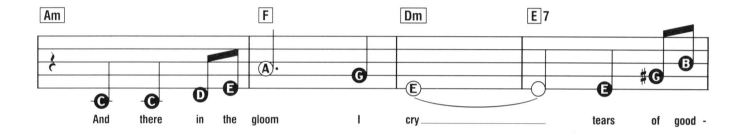

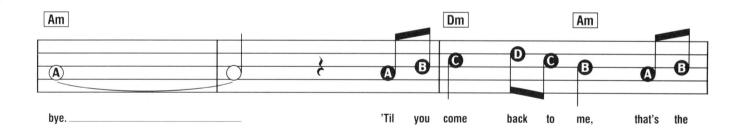

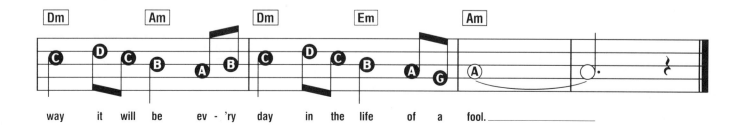

MARCH

Other appropriate rhythms are Fox Trot and Polka.

Many marches, though not ''Anchors Aweigh,'' are written in 6/8 time. In such cases, a 6/8 march is required for the accompaniment. In the event your keyboard doesn't have this rhythm, you can substitute the waltz rhythm at a fast tempo.

Anchors Aweigh

Regi-Sound Program: 2
Rhythm: March

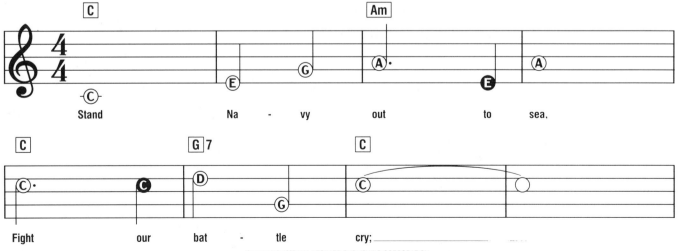

SLOW ROCK

Other appropriate rhythms are Rock, Jazz Rock and 8 Beat.

The cymbal part of the Slow Rock rhythm is in a triplet pattern. The illustration shows how this pattern and the first two measures of the song relate.

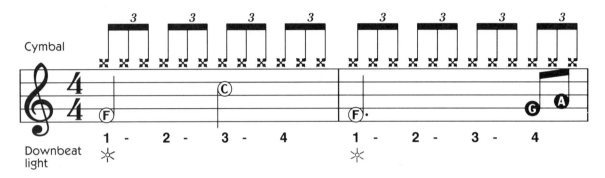

To get the feel of this rhythm, play the entire melody with the drums, omitting the chords. Once you're comfortable, put it all together.

The arpeggio feature is an effective background for the Slow Rock rhythm.

Can't Help Falling In Love

Regi-Sound Program: 7
Rhythm: Slow Rock

Words and Music by George David Weiss,
Hugo Peretti, and Luigi Creatore

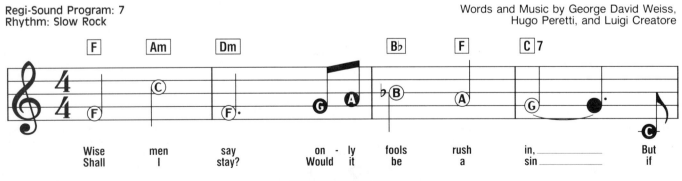

RHUMBA

Other appropriate rhythms are Latin, Beguine and Bossa Nova.

New Note:
Low G

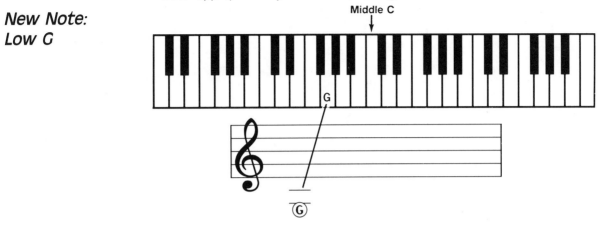

If your keyboard has a Marimba voice with a repeating effect, it would work well in this song.

More
(Theme From MONDO CANE)

Regi-Sound Program: 10
Rhythm: Rhumba

English Words by Norman Newell
Music by Riz Ortolani and Nino Oliviero

SWING

Other appropriate rhythms are Fox Trot, Ballad and Big Band.

Start up the drums and play just the melody, counting as you play. Before putting it all together, use the full accompaniment and hum or sing the melody.

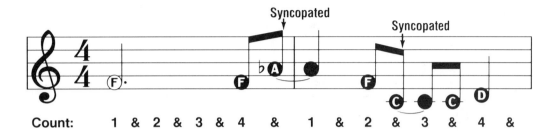

Count: 1 & 2 & 3 & 4 & 1 & 2 & 3 & 4 &

Tuxedo Junction

Words by Buddy Feyne
Music by Erskine Hawkins, William Johnson
and Julian Dash

Regi-Sound Program: 7
Rhythm: Swing

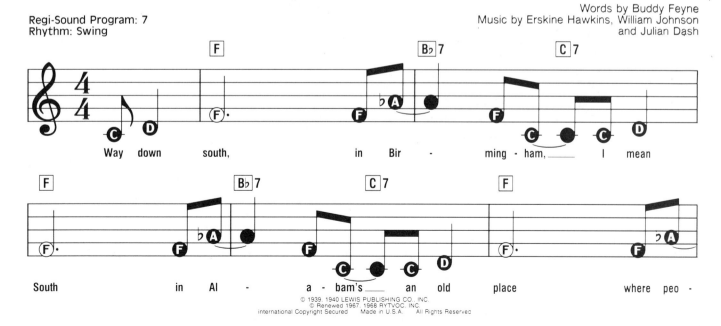

Way down south, in Bir - ming-ham,____ I mean

South in Al - a - bam's____ an old place where peo -

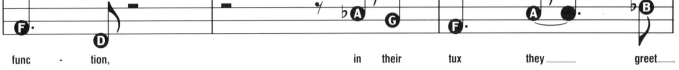

func - tion,   in their   tux   they_____   greet____

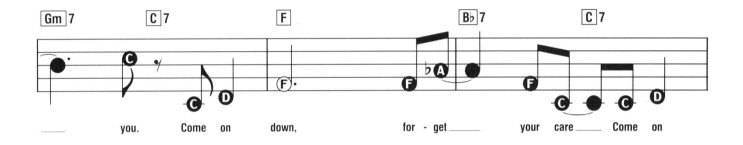

_____   you.   Come   on   down,   for - get_____   your   care _____   Come   on

down,   you'll   find_____   me   there. _____   So   long   town!   I'm   head -

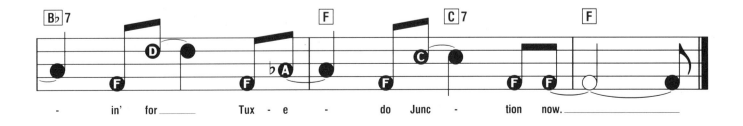

- in'   for_____   Tux - e -   do   Junc -   tion   now._____

WALTZ

"Oh, What A Beautiful Mornin'," like most Broadway show tunes, has two distinct sections — the verse and the refrain (chorus).

The verse is a sung introduction that is often played without a specific tempo (ad lib). The refrain, on the other hand, is the main part of the tune, which is normally played in tempo. The verse and refrain sections are marked in your music. For the verse, play accompaniment without rhythm, if possible; then, activate the waltz rhythm as indicated at the refrain.

Oh, What A Beautiful Mornin'
(From "OKLAHOMA")

Regi-Sound Program: 10
Rhythm: Waltz

Words by Oscar Hammerstein II
Music by Richard Rodgers

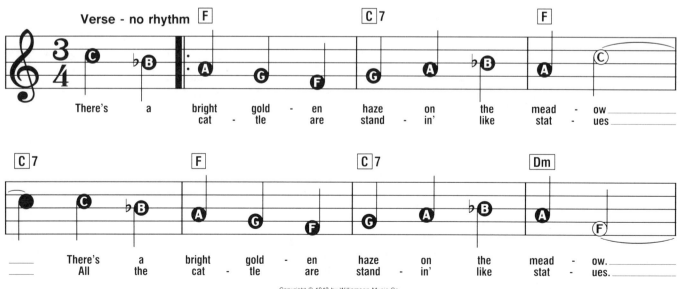

SAMBA

Other appropriate rhythms are Latin, Bossa Nova, Salsa and Reggae.

An extended ending based on a pattern of chord changes is often used by musicians to improvise on for an exciting finish. The chord changes for this ending are alternate measures of C and Bb. The first two-measure pattern you play replaces the existing last two measures of the song. Here are some suggestions:

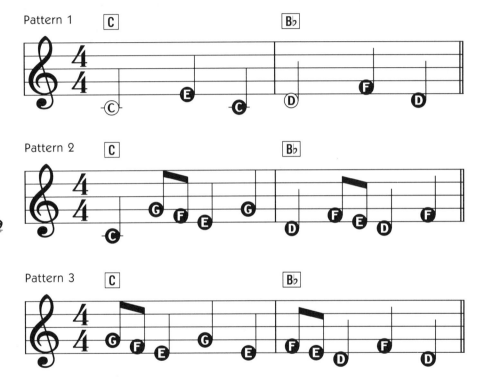

How to proceed:

- Play each of the two-measure patterns until you are familiar with them.

- Now, when you get to the last two measures of the song, begin playing any of the three patterns. Play each pattern as long as you wish. Omit any you wish.

- When you want to end the song, play a C note and gradually fade.

- Finally, how about developing some patterns of your own!

Samba De Orfeu

Regi-Sound Program: 2
Rhythm: Samba

Words by Antonio Maria
Music by Luiz Bonfa

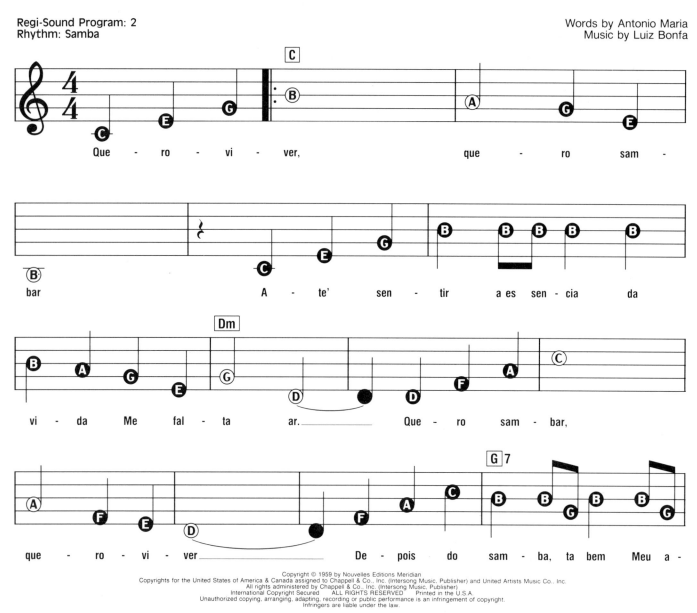

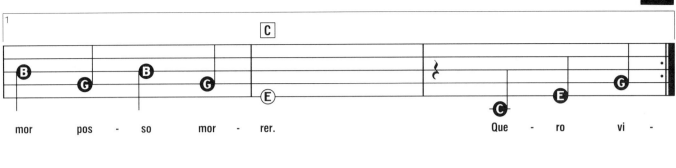

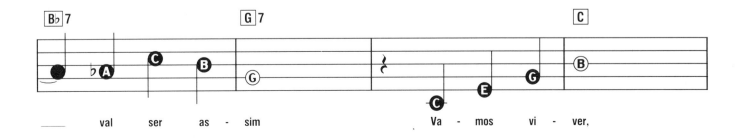

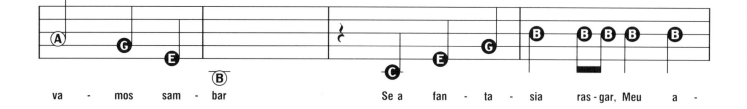

va - mos sam - bar   Se a fan - ta - sia ras-gar, Meu a -

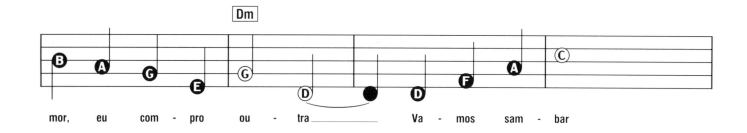

mor, eu com - pro ou - tra_____ Va - mos sam - bar

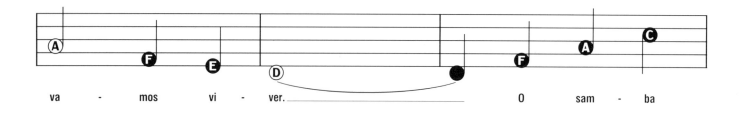

va - mos vi - ver._____ O sam - ba

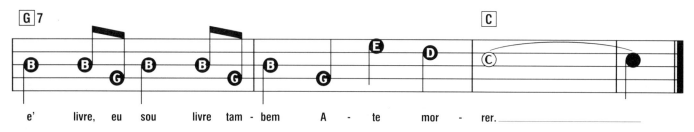

e' livre, eu sou livre tam - bem A - te mor - rer._____

COUNTRY

Other appropriate rhythms are Fox Trot, Shuffle, Slow Rock and Ballad.

If your keyboard has a fill feature, you know that fills can be programmed automatically. The following examples are a few fills that you can play yourself in "Green Green Grass Of Home."

Green Green Grass Of Home

Regi-Sound Program: 8
Rhythm: Country

Words and Music by
Curly Putman

NO RHYTHM

Sustained accompaniment often is most effective for hymns, Christmas carols and folk music. In this instance, turn off the drums. Without the rhythm playing, you can change chords on any beat and not be concerned about how the rhythm is going to fit.

Part 2 on the next page is included in the event your keyboard has a sequencer. (Refer to page 13 for basic information about sequencers.) In this case, choose the part or parts you want to play and sequence the rest. Consult your owner's manual for details.

Part 1 — Melody And Chords

America

Regi-Sound Program: 5
No Rhythm

Part 2 — Harmony

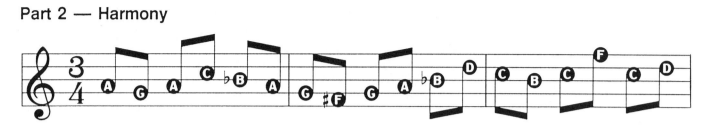

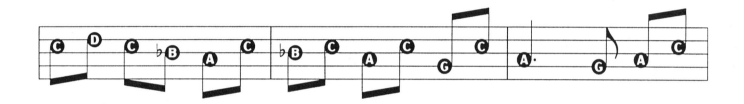

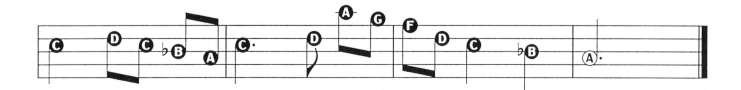

ROCK

Other appropriate rhythms are Jazz Rock, Funk Rock, Disco, 8 Beat, 16 Beat and Fusion.

Rhythm Changes

Changing rhythms is an excellent way to add interest to your playing. Keep in mind that the rhythm should remain steady. In other words, don't add extra beats in a measure just to make the change. Write rhythm changes in your music a couple of measures before they occur, so you can think ahead. Sometimes, you can gain the time needed to press a new rhythm control by "borrowing" a few beats from a long melody note. Watch for the rhythm changes in "Just The Way You Are."

Just The Way You Are

Regi-Sound Program: 7
Rhythm: Rock

Words and Music by
Billy Joel

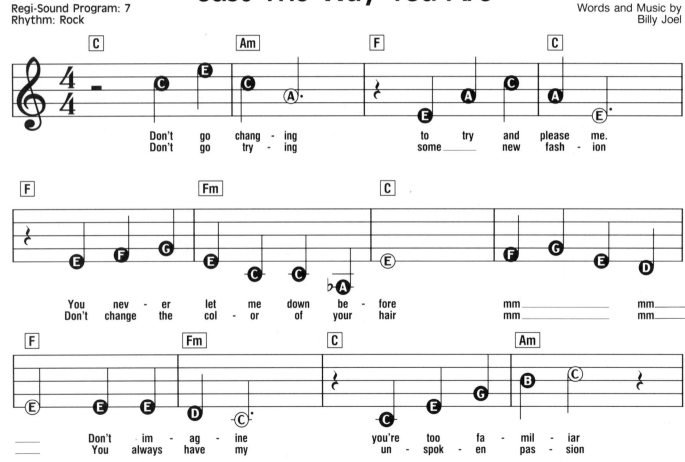

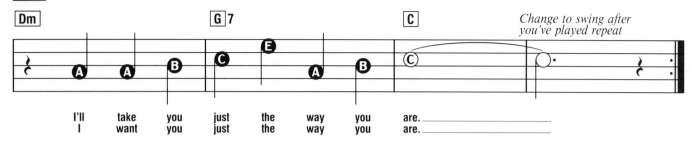

Change to swing after you've played repeat

I'll take you just the way you are. _____
I want you just the way you are. _____

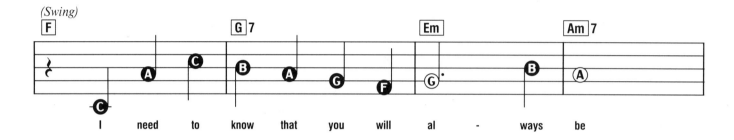

(Swing)

I need to know that you will al - ways be

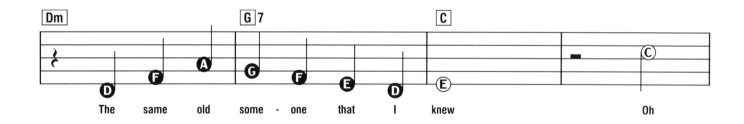

The same old some - one that I knew   Oh

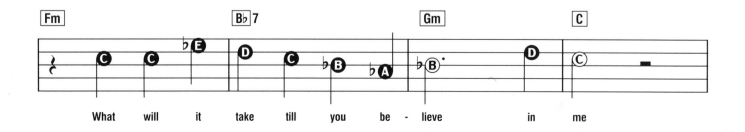

What will it take till you be - lieve in me

PART THREE

How many times have you sat at your keyboard and thought, "How can I do more when I play?" or "What makes the pros sound so good?"

Part Three of INSTANT KEYBOARD answers these questions by showing you some simple techniques that you can work into your playing to make each song your own. Many of the "tricks" that professional players use are not difficult; in fact, some of them are extremely easy. What separates most professionals from everyone else is knowing which technique to use, and where to use it. Once you know how to do this, you can apply these techniques to all of the music you play.

The suggested techniques are printed in gray. This enables you to easily focus on each technique and quickly learn the best places to use them. You'll find it helpful to play through each basic arrangement before you attempt to add the gray notes. This will enable you to become familiar with each song, and allow you to better hear the effects of using the various techniques.

8va, Loco

One of the easiest ways to change the arrangement of a song is to play parts of it in different octaves. An octave is the distance from any key to the next key having the same name — C to C, for example. Count the white keys from one C key to the next, up or down the keyboard, and you'll find the number is eight; octave comes from an Italian word meaning "eight."

In the music notation, octave is abbreviated 8va. When you see this symbol above the staff, play the notes an octave (eight notes) higher than where they're written. If the effect is to last a short time (a few notes or a few measures), the 8va is followed by a broken line, showing you how long to continue playing an octave higher. When the effect is to last for a line or two of music, or longer, the symbol **loco** appears where the 8va is to be cancelled. This Italian word means "at the written pitch," telling you to play the notes where they are written.

To reinforce playing notes an octave higher, locate and play the notes in the illustration.

Written:

Played:

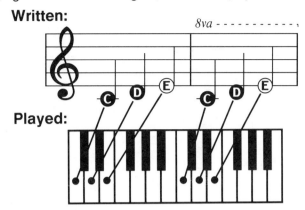

In most cases, you'll find that octave changes in this book occur between sections of songs.

Longer

Regi-Sound Program: 2
Rhythm: Rock

Words and Music by
Dan Fogelberg

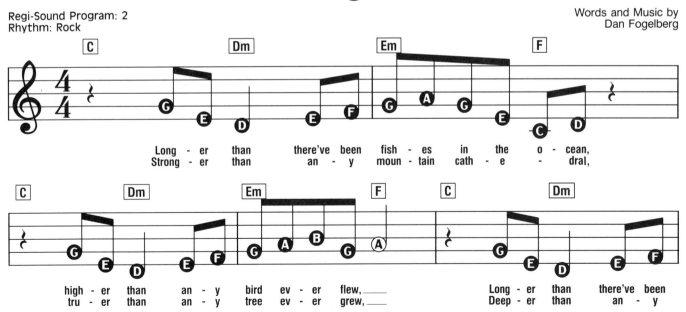

Long - er   than   there've been   fish - es   in   the   o - cean,
Strong - er   than   an - y   moun - tain   cath - e - dral,

high - er   than   an - y   bird   ev - er   flew, ____
tru - er   than   an - y   tree   ev - er   grew, ____

Long - er   than   there've been
Deep - er   than   an - y

8va Lower

This symbol tells you to play the notes an octave **lower** then where they're written. The broken lines and **loco** also occur as described earlier.

Written:

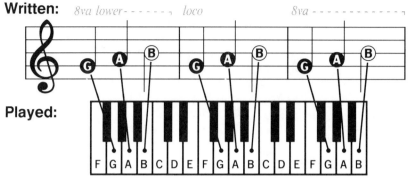

Played:

An optional effect appears in the beginning of "At The Hop." If you spend a little time practicing it, you'll find that it makes a good introduction. Just play and hold each key as you add the next one; the fingering is suggested to help you.

At The Hop

Regi-Sound Program: 8
Rhythm: Rock

Words and Music by Arthur Singer,
John Medora and David White

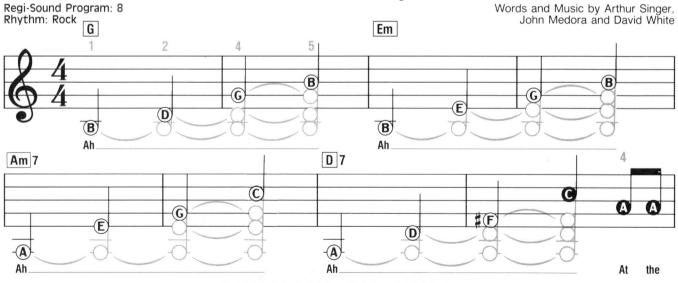

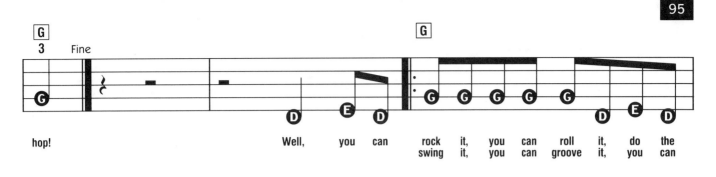

hop!   Well, you can   rock it, you can   roll it, do the
                                 swing it, you can   groove it, you can

stomp and   e - ven stroll it at the hop.   When the
real - ly   start to move it   at the hop.   Where the

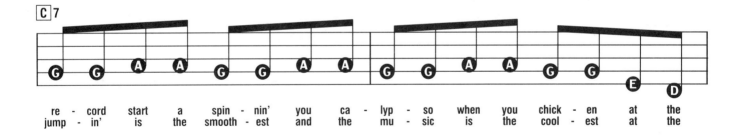

re - cord   start   a   spin - nin' you   ca - lyp - so when you   chick - en at   the
jump - in'   is   the   smooth - est and   the mu - sic is the   cool - est at   the

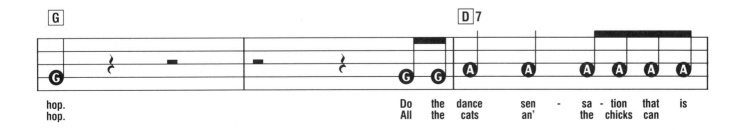

hop.   Do   the   dance   sen -   sa - tion that is
hop.   All the   cats   an'   the chicks can

96

Changing Regi-Sound Programs

Another easy way to personalize an arrangement is to change keyboard voices while you play. It doesn't require any additional playing ability; rather, you must have a good feel for the song — the kind of tune it is, the mood it creates, the tempo — and then plan your voices accordingly. You might want to start light (solo flute, piano, etc.) and build to a big finish (brass, ensemble organ sound, etc.), or start at a medium level (strings, for example), lighten up to a solo sound, and then finish the way you started, or maybe with an even bigger sound. AL-WAYS consider the song and what it suggests.

Ease of changing Regi-Sound Programs while you play will depend on the particular keyboard model you're playing — you may have to push only one button, or as many as two or three. Refer to the Regi-Sound Programs guide found in the back of this book to determine how the Regi-Sound numbers relate to the voices on your keyboard. The ideal places to change are between sections of a song; it's helpful if there are rests in the melody, or longer melody notes. Keep the following points in mind as you play:

- Changes should reflect the mood of the song.

- Changes should generally be obvious — contrast sounds **tastefully**.

- Think ahead; prepare for a change a few measures in advance.

- Keep the rhythm constant. Don't add extra beats just to make changes.

- At the point of change, decide how much time you have and make no more changes than possible in that time. If necessary, "steal" beats from a longer melody note to provide time to make changes. The following example, from "The Rainbow Connection," illustrates:

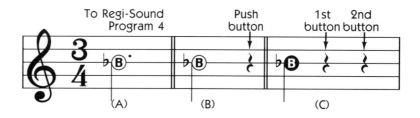

If your keyboard has a memory feature to work with the accompaniment, the accompaniment chord will keep playing even if you use your left hand to change voices, while your right hand holds the melody note (as in A). B and C show how to rob beats from the melody note if you must use your right hand to make changes, while your left hand is holding down the chord key.

The Rainbow Connection

Regi-Sound Program: 4
Rhythm: Waltz

By Paul Williams
and Kenneth L. Ascher

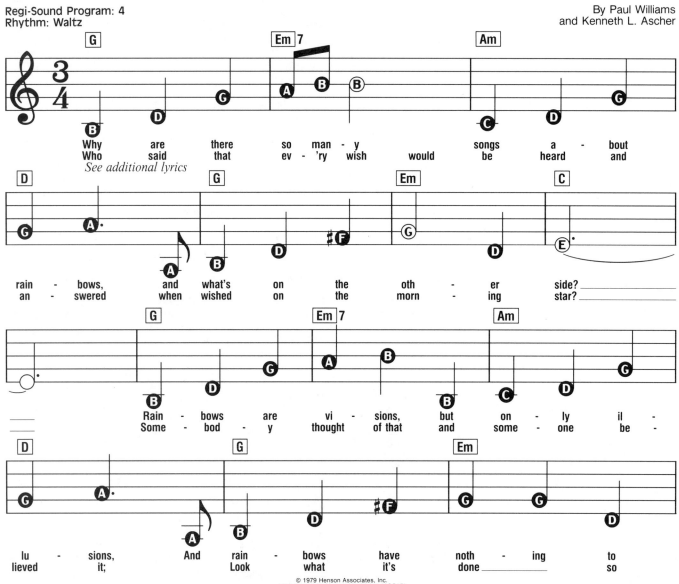

See additional lyrics

Why are there so man - y songs a - bout
Who said that ev - 'ry wish would be heard and

rain - bows, and what's on the oth - er side? _____
an - swered when wished on the morn - ing star? _____

_____ Rain - bows are vi - sions, but on - ly il -
_____ Some - bod - y thought of that and some - one be -

lu - sions, And rain - bows have noth - ing to
lieved it; Look what it's done _____ so

100

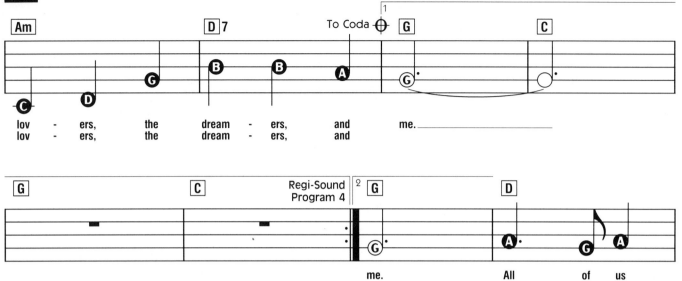

lov - ers, the dream - ers, and me.
lov - ers, the dream - ers, and

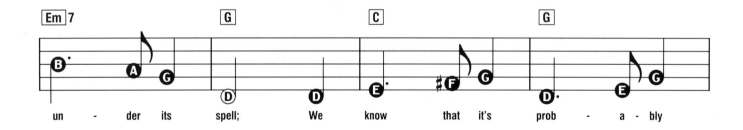

me. All of us

Em 7   G   C   G

un - der its spell; We know that it's prob - a - bly

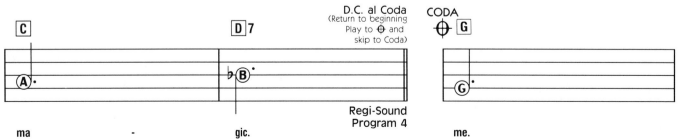

ma - gic.

me.

8va to end.

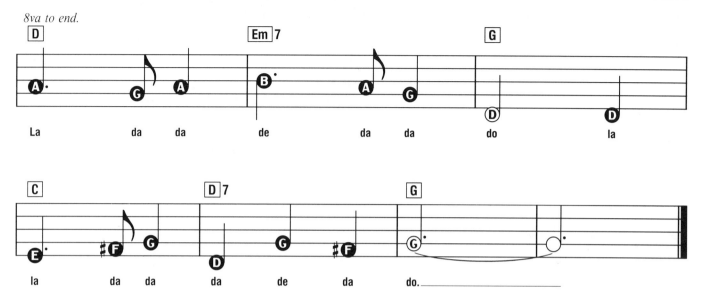

La   da   da   de   da   da   do   la

la   da   da   da   de   da   do.

Additional Lyrics

Have you been half asleep and have you heard voices?
I've heard them calling my name.
Is this the sweet sound that calls the young sailors?
The voice might be one and the same.

I've heard it too many times to ignore it.
It's something that I'm s'posed to be.
Someday we'll find it, the rainbow connection;
The lovers, the dreamers, and me.

To Coda

Somewhere Out There

(From "An American Tail")

Regi-Sound Program: 7
Rhythm: Rock

By James Horner, Barry Mann
and Cynthia Weil

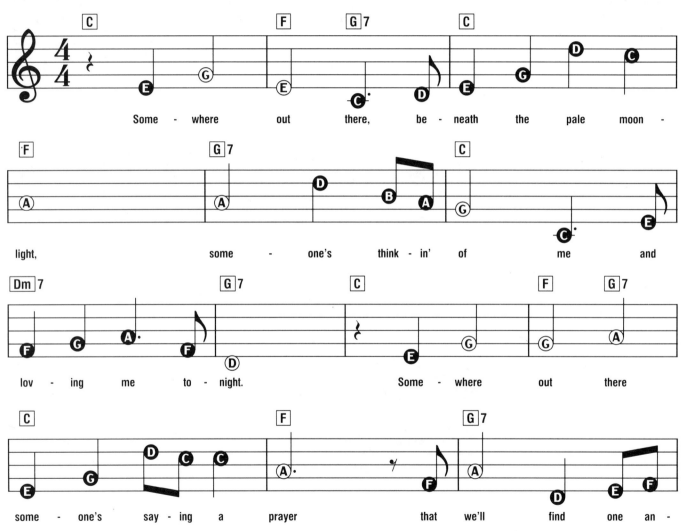

Regi-Sound Program: 8

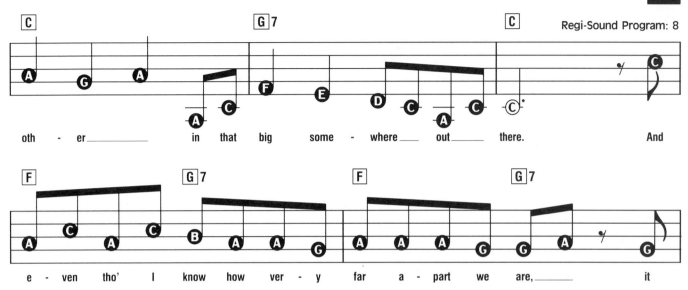

oth - er ___ in that big some - where ___ out ___ there. And

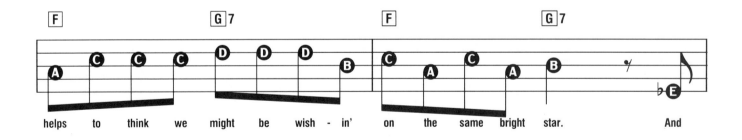

e - ven tho' I know how ver - y far a - part we are, ___ it

helps to think we might be wish - in' on the same bright star. And

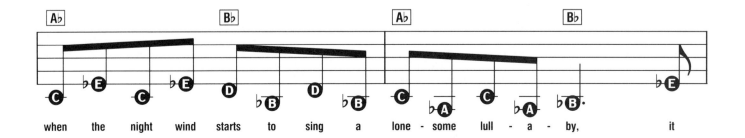

when the night wind starts to sing a lone - some lull - a - by, it

Regi-Sound
Program: 7

helps to think we're sleep - ing un - der - neath the same big sky.

Some - where out there, if love can see us through,

then we'll be to - geth - er some - where out there, out where dreams come

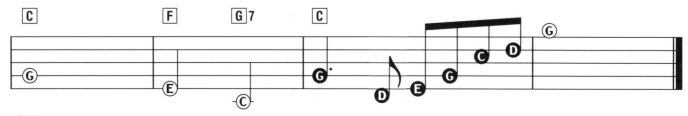

true.

Grace Notes

A **grace note** is an ornamental note, played quickly, which has no time value of its own. It takes its value from either the note just before it or just after it. To show that they're not counted in the total number of beats in a measure, grace notes always appear in smaller-than-standard-notation — of course, the ones in this book appear gray.

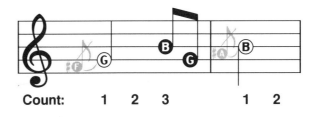

Grace notes can be used to decorate your playing, as you'll see in the next few songs. While we show many examples, use the ones you like (after trying them all). An important point to keep in mind about grace notes (and most other effects and techniques) is to treat them like spices in cooking — USE THEM SPARINGLY! Tastefully placed grace notes add style and professionalism to your playing.

''Amazing Grace'' uses single grace notes, all coming from below the melody note. They can come from above, as well. ''Till'' uses double and triple grace notes from above and below.

Amazing Grace

Regi-Sound Program: 7
Rhythm: Waltz

Words by John Newton
Early American Melody

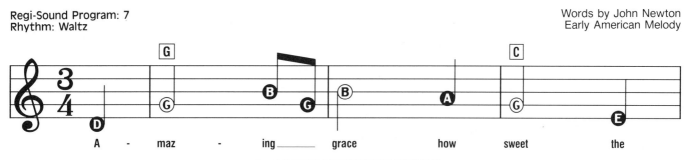

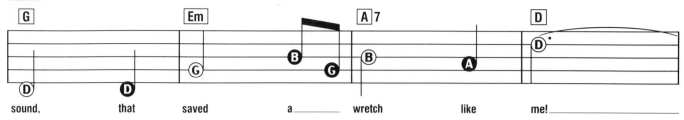

sound,   that   saved   a ____ wretch   like   me! ____

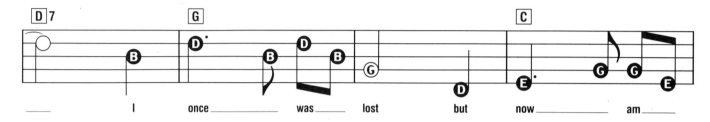

____ I   once ____ was ____ lost   but   now ____ am ____

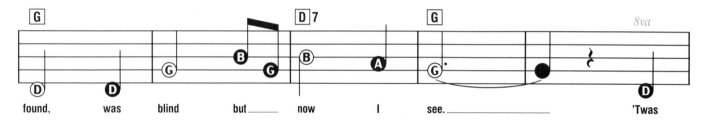

found,   was   blind   but ____ now   I   see. ____ 'Twas

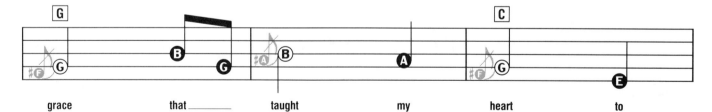

grace   that ____ taught   my   heart   to

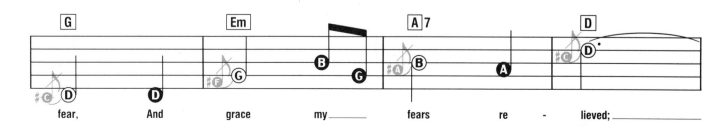

fear,   And   grace   my ____ fears   re - lieved; ____

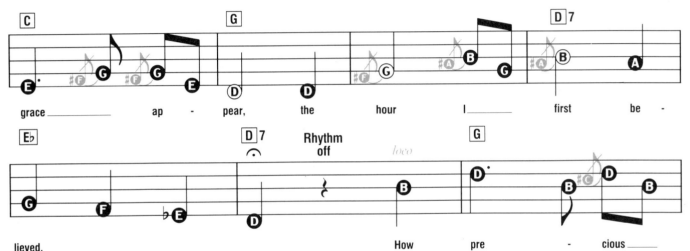

How pre - cious ____ did that grace ____ ap - pear, the hour I ____ first be -

lieved. How pre - cious ____

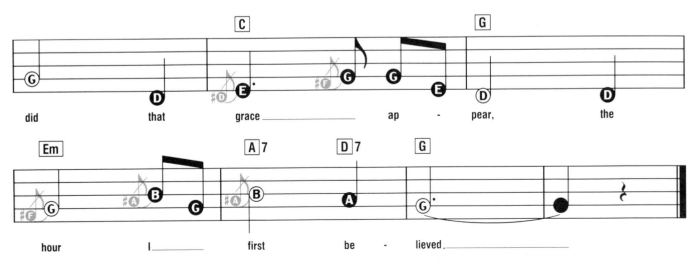

did that grace ____ ap - pear, the hour I ____ first be - lieved. ____

Till

Regi-Sound Program: 1
Rhythm: Rock

Words by Carl Sigman
Music by Charles Danvers

Ornaments

In this book, the word **ornament** applies to various figures used to decorate a melody; ornaments are the next logical step after grace notes. One type of ornament uses the melody note and the note either just **above** or just **below** the melody note (called **neighbor notes**). The illustration compares grace notes, upper neighbor ornaments, and lower neighbor ornaments.

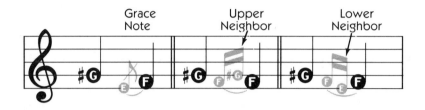

Whether you use ornaments with upper or lower neighbors is your choice. Sometimes one will sound better than the other; other times, it's a matter of which is easiest to play. We preferred ornaments with upper neighbors in the arrangement of "Havah Nagilah."

Havah Nagilah

Regi-Sound Program: 5
Rhythm: March

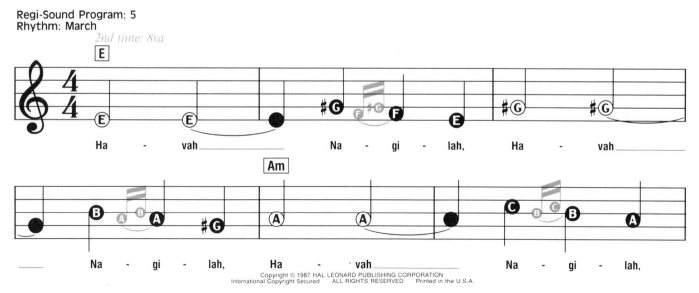

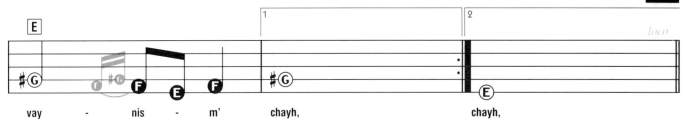

vay - nis - m' chayh, chayh,

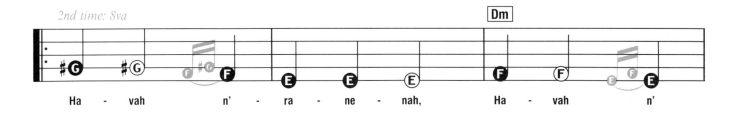

Ha - vah n' - ra - ne - nah, Ha - vah n'

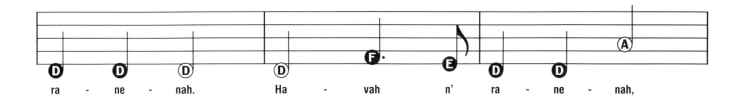

ra - ne - nah. Ha - vah n' ra - ne - nah,

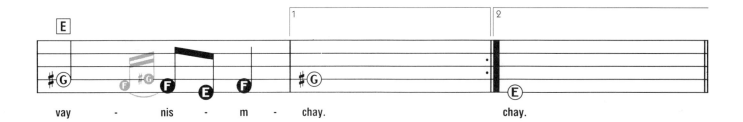

vay - nis - m - chay. chay.

Melodic Fills

A **melodic fill**, as the name suggests, is a group of notes that fills in around the melody. While grace notes and other ornaments are melodic fills, they are quickly-played, lacy figures which decorate the melody. The melodic fills discussed here generally take their place along with the original melody notes of the song involved. They are not necessarily played more quickly; therefore, while they're gray in color, they are not smaller in size as are grace and other ornaments.

Melodic fills are used to fill time/space between melody notes; you might think of them as **melodic connectors**. In the Beatles' hit, ''And I Love Her,'' the fills appear as eighth notes, sixteenth notes, and various triplets. Toward the end of the second page, a different kind of melodic fill occurs: each melody note is played and held until all three are sounding. This effect is worth trying whenever the melody moves in small skips as it does in this particular measure. It's the same effect used in ''At The Hop.''

Sixteenth Notes

You'll be introduced to a new note value — the **sixteenth note**, and **triplets**. The sixteenth note receives ¼ count. Therefore, it takes four sixteenth notes to equal one count.

Triplets

A **triplet** indicates that you play three notes in the same amount of time it would normally take to play two notes of the same type.

1 count   2 counts

And I Love Her

Regi-Sound Program: 8
Rhythm: Rock or Jazz Rock

Words and Music by
John Lennon and Paul McCartney

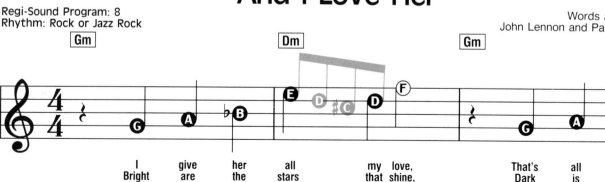

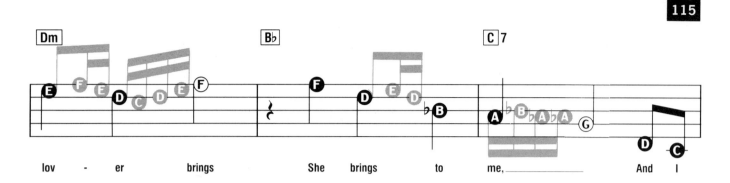

lov - er brings   She brings to me,_____ And I

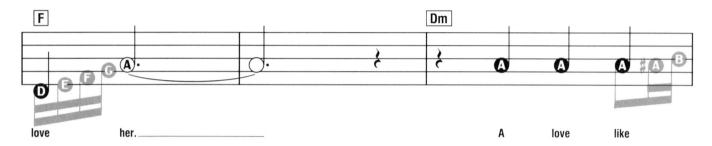

love her._____   A love like

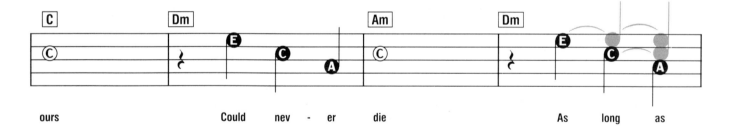

ours   Could nev - er die   As long as

D.C. al Fine
(Return to beginning
and play to Fine)

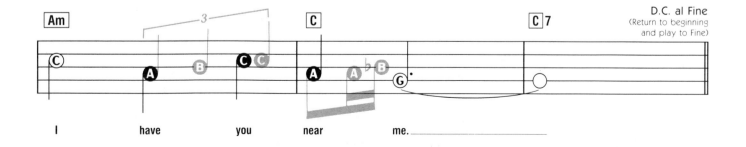

I have you near me._____

Because "Mickey Mouse March" is in 6/8 time, most of the fills reflect the triplet feel. In the **bridge**, or middle section of the song, a different style of fill is used: play and hold the melody note with your fourth or fifth finger, and reach down and play the "answering" notes below it — all with your right hand! If your keyboard is playable without the auto rhythm, try the optional ending, reminiscent of the one used on the Mousketeers TV show.

Mickey Mouse March

Regi-Sound Program: 5
Rhythm: 6/8 March

Words and Music by
Jimmie Dodd

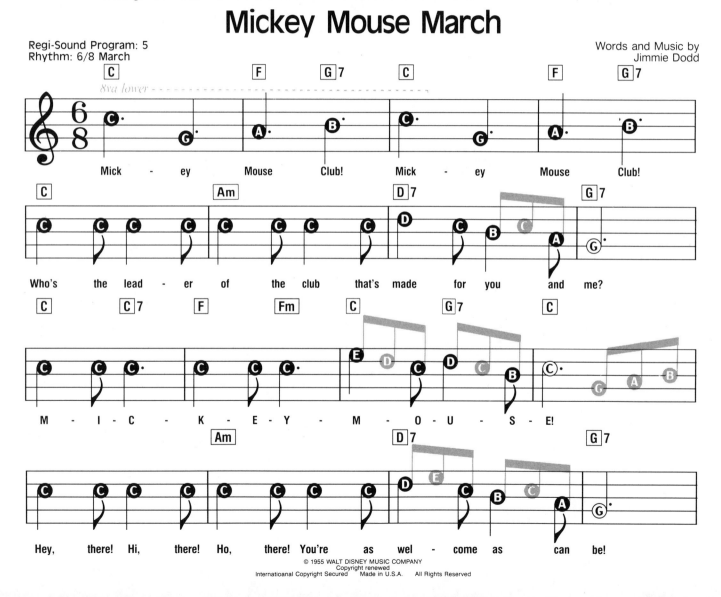

The Rolling Stones' "As Tears Go By" presents a review of the playing techniques you've learned up to now, with some elaboration. There are a number of measures where independent fill notes are played while a melody note is held. In measure 7, you can either hold the F and play the optional notes, or play the entire measure as eighth notes only.

As Tears Go By

Regi-Sound Program: 4
Rhythm: Rock

Words and Music by Mick Jagger,
Keith Richard and Andrew Loog Oldham

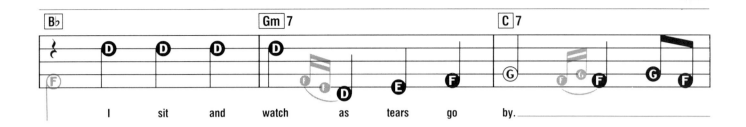

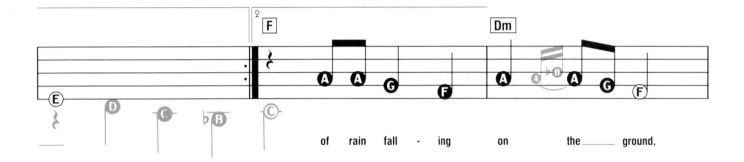

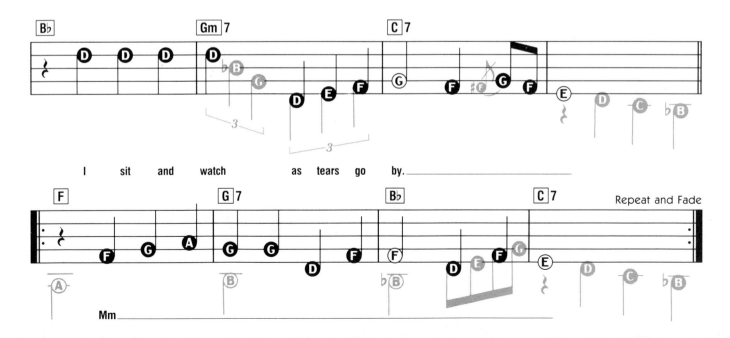

CHORD CHARTS

PART FOUR

Fingered Chords

Most keyboards provide two ways of playing chords — **1-Finger Chords** and **Fingered Chords**. Fingered Chords, and how to play them, are the subject of Part Four. In the fingered chord mode, you play all the notes of the chord in the easy play section of the keyboard instead of just one or two keys.

The Fingered Chord you play automatically provides an appropriate bass. The chord and bass then play in the style of the automatic rhythm you've chosen.

The chords in the chord charts that follow are made up of three or four notes. The notes that make up a chord determine the kind of chord that it is. Major and minor chords are three-note chords, while seventh and minor seventh chords are four-note chords.

All chords are built upon a note called the **root**. The root is the main tone of the bass and gives the chord its letter name. For example, a C major chord (abbreviated C) and a C minor chord (abbreviated Cm) both have the note C as their root. When a chord is played with the root (letter-name) note on the bottom, it is said to be in **root position**.

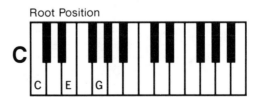

Root Position

Inversions

The notes of a chord can also be played in different orders, called **inversions**.

First Inversion

C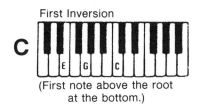

(First note above the root
at the bottom.)

Second Inversion

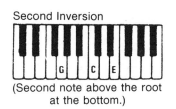

(Second note above the root
at the bottom.)

Seventh chords and minor seventh chords have four notes instead of three. The additional note provides an additional inversion. The third note above the root is on the bottom of the chord.

Root Position

C7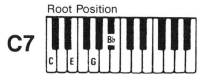

First Inversion

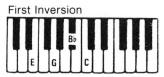

(First note above the root
at the bottom.)

Second Inversion

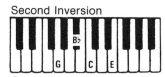

(Second note above the root
at the bottom.)

Third Inversion

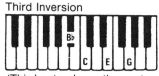

(Third note above the root
at the bottom.)

Root Position

Cm7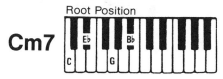

First Inversion

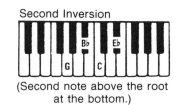

(First note above the root
at the bottom.)

Second Inversion

(Second note above the root
at the bottom.)

Third Inversion

(Third note above the root
at the bottom.)

The most commonly played positions for all chords are shaded in the chord charts.

C CHORDS

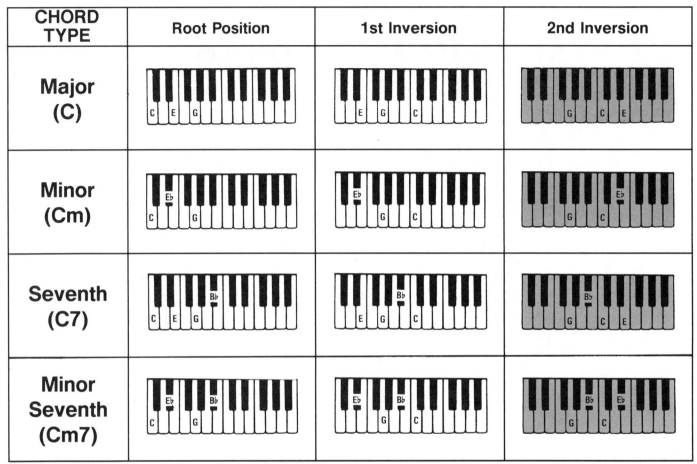

CHORD TYPE	Root Position	1st Inversion	2nd Inversion
Major (C)	C E G	E G C	G C E
Minor (Cm)	C Eb G	Eb G C	G C Eb
Seventh (C7)	C E G Bb	E G Bb C	G Bb C E
Minor Seventh (Cm7)	C Eb G Bb	Eb G Bb C	G Bb C Eb

C7 — 3rd Inversion

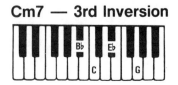

Bb C E G

Cm7 — 3rd Inversion

Bb Eb C G

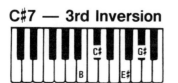

C#/Db CHORDS

CHORD TYPE	Root Position	1st Inversion	2nd Inversion
Major (C#/Db)	C# G# E#	G# C# E#	G# C# E#
Minor (C#/Dbm)	C# G# E	G# C# E	G# C# E
Seventh (C#/Db7)	C# G# E# B	G# C# E# B	G# C# B E#
Minor Seventh (C#/Dbm7)	C# G# E B	G# C# E B	G# C# B E

C#7 — 3rd Inversion

C# G# B E#

C#m7 — 3rd Inversion

C# G# B E

D CHORDS

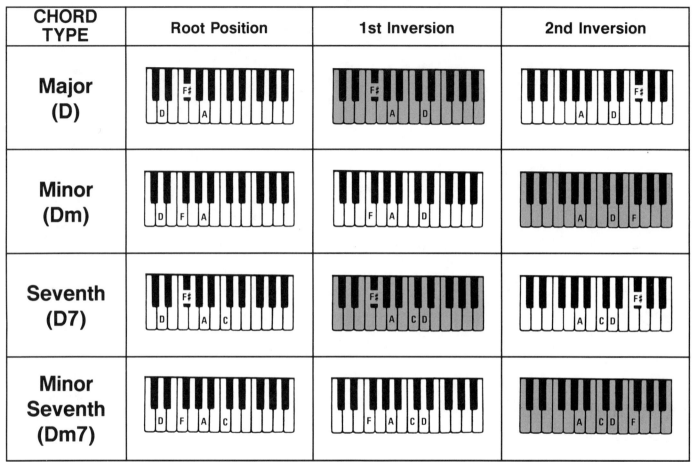

CHORD TYPE	Root Position	1st Inversion	2nd Inversion
Major (D)			
Minor (Dm)			
Seventh (D7)			
Minor Seventh (Dm7)			

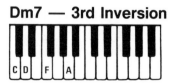

D7 — 3rd Inversion

Dm7 — 3rd Inversion

E♭ CHORDS

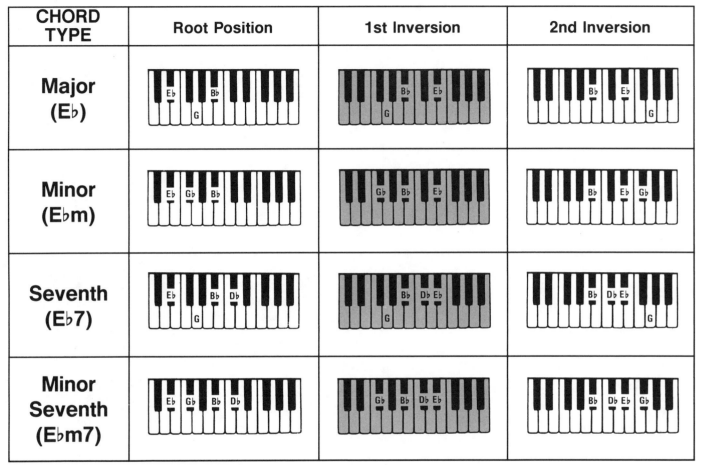

CHORD TYPE	Root Position	1st Inversion	2nd Inversion
Major (E♭)	E♭ G B♭	G B♭ E♭	B♭ E♭ G
Minor (E♭m)	E♭ G♭ B♭	G♭ B♭ E♭	B♭ E♭ G♭
Seventh (E♭7)	E♭ G B♭ D♭	G B♭ D♭ E♭	B♭ D♭ E♭ G
Minor Seventh (E♭m7)	E♭ G♭ B♭ D♭	G♭ B♭ D♭ E♭	B♭ D♭ E♭ G♭

E♭7 — 3rd Inversion

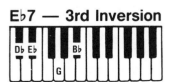

E♭m7 — 3rd Inversion

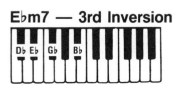

E CHORDS

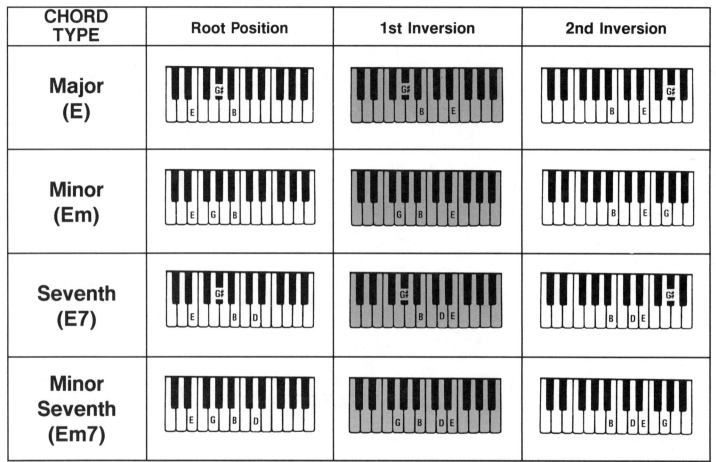

CHORD TYPE	Root Position	1st Inversion	2nd Inversion
Major (E)	E — G# — B	G# — B — E	B — E — G#
Minor (Em)	E — G — B	G — B — E	B — E — G
Seventh (E7)	E — G# — B — D	G# — B — D — E	B — D — E — G#
Minor Seventh (Em7)	E — G — B — D	G — B — D — E	B — D — E — G

E7 — 3rd Inversion

Em7 — 3rd Inversion

F CHORDS

CHORD TYPE	Root Position	1st Inversion	2nd Inversion
Major (F)			
Minor (Fm)			
Seventh (F7)			
Minor Seventh (Fm7)			

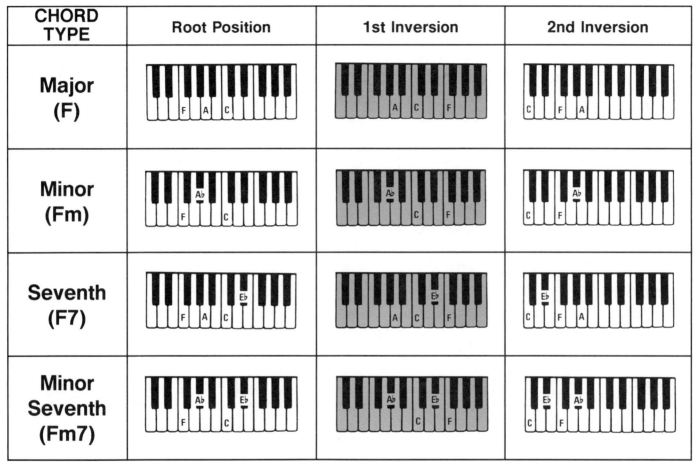

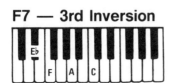

F7 — 3rd Inversion

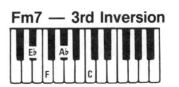

Fm7 — 3rd Inversion

F#/Gb CHORDS

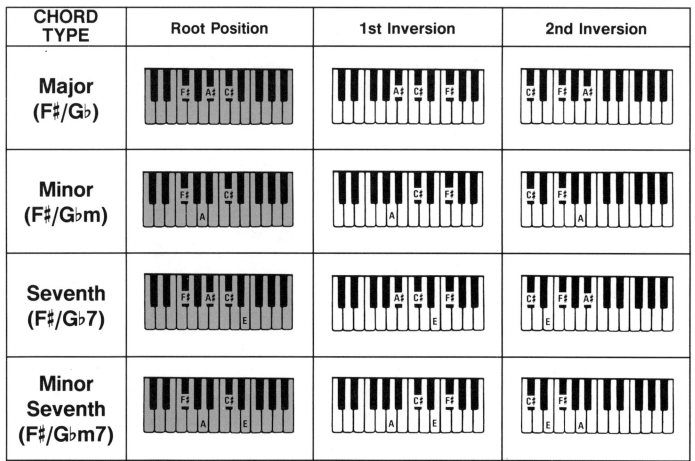

CHORD TYPE	Root Position	1st Inversion	2nd Inversion
Major (F#/Gb)	F# A# C#	A# C# F#	C# F# A#
Minor (F#/Gbm)	F# C# A	C# F# A	C# F# A
Seventh (F#/Gb7)	F# A# C# E	A# C# F# E	C# F# A# E
Minor Seventh (F#/Gbm7)	F# C# A E	C# F# A E	C# F# E A

F#/Gb7 — 3rd Inversion

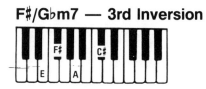

F#/Gbm7 — 3rd Inversion

G CHORDS

CHORD TYPE	Root Position	1st Inversion	2nd Inversion
Major (G)	G B D	B D G	D G B
Minor (Gm)	G Bb D	Bb D G	D G Bb
Seventh (G7)	G B D F	B D F G	D F G B
Minor Seventh (Gm7)	G Bb D F	Bb D F G	D F G Bb

G7 — 3rd Inversion

F G B D

Gm7 — 3rd Inversion

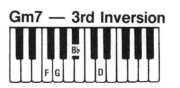

F G Bb D

Ab CHORDS

CHORD TYPE	Root Position	1st Inversion	2nd Inversion
Major (Ab)			
Minor (Abm)			
Seventh (Ab7)			
Minor Seventh (Abm7)			

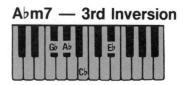

Ab7 — 3rd Inversion   **Abm7 — 3rd Inversion**

A CHORDS

CHORD TYPE	Root Position	1st Inversion	2nd Inversion
Major (A)	C# A E	C# E A	C# E A
Minor (Am)	A C E	C E A	E A C
Seventh (A7)	C# A E G	C# E G A	C# E G A
Minor Seventh (Am7)	A C E G	C E G A	E G A C

A7 — 3rd Inversion

Am7 — 3rd Inversion

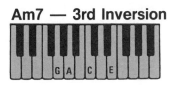

B♭ CHORDS

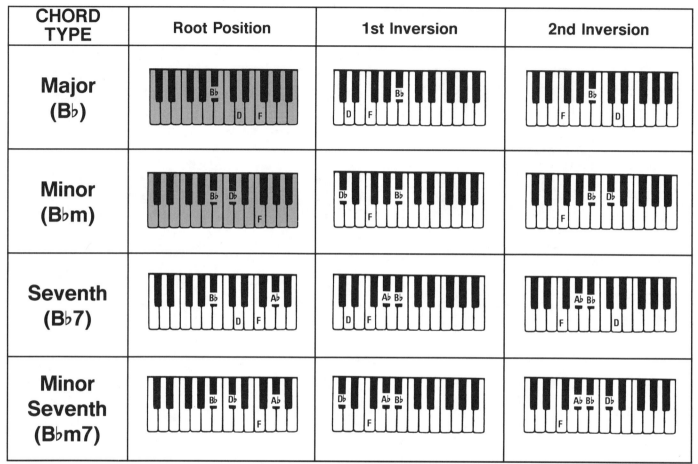

CHORD TYPE	Root Position	1st Inversion	2nd Inversion
Major (B♭)	B♭ D F	D F B♭	F B♭ D
Minor (B♭m)	B♭ D♭ F	D♭ F B♭	F B♭ D♭
Seventh (B♭7)	B♭ D F A♭	D F A♭ B♭	A♭ B♭ F D
Minor Seventh (B♭m7)	B♭ D♭ F A♭	D♭ F A♭ B♭	A♭ B♭ D♭ F

B♭7 — 3rd Inversion

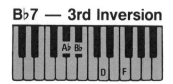

B♭m7 — 3rd Inversion

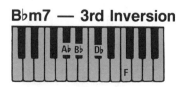

B CHORDS

CHORD TYPE	Root Position	1st Inversion	2nd Inversion
Major (B)	D# F# B	D# F# B	F# D# B
Minor (Bm)	F# B D#	F# D B	F# B D
Seventh (B7)	D# F# B A	D# F# A B	F# D# A B
Minor Seventh (Bm7)	F# B D# A	F# D A B	F# A B D

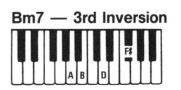

B7 — 3rd Inversion

A B D# F#

Bm7 — 3rd Inversion

A B D F#

Regi-Sound Programs

Regi-Sound Program	
1	Flute, Tibia, Piccolo, Clarinet, Organ 1, Jazz Organ
2	Full Tibias, Jazz Flute, Clarinet, Organ, Elec. Organ, Organ 2
3	Violin, Cello, String(s), Accordion, Diapason
4	Trumpet, Brass, Oboe, Accordion, Guitar, Hawaiian Guitar, Jazz Organ
5	Trumpet, Brass, Horn, Clarinet, Organ
6	Organ, Pipe Organ, Harpsichord
7	Vibraphone, Vibes, Jazz Organ, Organ, Elec. Piano, Piano, Guitar
8	Piano
9	Trumpet, Clarinet, Oboe, Bassoon
10	Violin, String, Banjo, Marimba, Harpsichord

Index

About the Author

The best single word to describe Gary Meisner is "versatile." For the past fourteen years, he has been on the editorial staff of Hal Leonard Publishing Corporation, writing owner's manuals and educational programs for the major organ manufacturers, as well as editing piano materials and arranging songs for organ folios.

As an educator, Gary taught private music lessons, as well as elementary school, for twenty years before entering the publishing world.

Performing has always been an important part of his career. Niteclubs, show bands, radio, and television have all been included in his extensive list of performance credits.